D0722261

LITERATURE AND SCIENCE

LITERATURE AND SCIENCE

By

Aldous Huxley

1963

CHATTO & WINDUS

LONDON

PUBLISHED BY
Chatto & Windus Ltd
42 WILLIAM IV STREET
LONDON, W.C.2

*

Clarke, Irwin & Co. Ltd
TORONTO

Printed in Great Britain by T. & A. Constable Ltd
Hopetoun Street, Edinburgh

SNOW or Leavis? The bland scientism of *The Two Cultures or*, violent and ill-mannered, the one-track, moralistic literarism of the Richmond Lecture? If there were no other choice, we should indeed be badly off. But happily there are middle roads, there is a more realistic approach to the subject than was made by either of the two champions. And the two champions, let us remember, are not the only combatants in the field; they are merely, at this moment, the most notorious. The field has known a long succession of fighters for this cause or for that, a long succession, too, of earnest compromisers anxiously trying to negotiate a fruitful peace between the opposing forces, or at least a not too hostile symbiosis. One thinks of T. H. Huxley, with his advocacy of a primarily scientific education tempered (as Caltech, for example, and M.I.T. now temper it) with plenty of history, sociology, English literature and foreign languages. One thinks of Matthew Arnold, pleading for a primarily humanistic and specifically classical education, tempered by enough science to make its recipients understand the singularly un-Hellenic world in which they find themselves living. Huxley would most certainly have agreed with Arnold in thinking that man, and even man's remote ancestor, 'the hairy quadruped furnished with a tail and pointed ears, probably arboreal in his habits . . . carried hidden in his nature something destined to develop into a necessity for humane letters'. He refused, however, to accept 'the further conclusion that our hairy ancestor carried in his nature, also, a necessity for Greek', and would have

5

maintained instead, that this other spiritual necessity was for the methods and results of science.

Since the time, eighty years ago, of that famous argument between the chief representative of what Huxley called 'the Levites of culture' and the chief representative of 'what the poor humanist is sometimes apt to regard as its Nebuchadnezzars', much has been written on the themes of science versus humane letters, of science *and* humane letters. The most recent contributions to the argument have come from Professor Lionel Trilling and Dr Robert Oppenheimer. In an admirably judicious essay, published in the June 1962 issue of *Commentary*, Professor Trilling sums up the Leavis-Snow controversy and talks with subtlety and good sense about the relations between science, literature, culture and Mind. Dr Oppenheimer's paper, 'Science and Culture' appeared in *Encounter* for October 1962. It is a sound, but not particularly original essay; for in somewhat woollier language it says, more or less, what Eddington was saying in the thirties—what, indeed, any intelligent physicist, who also cares for the arts, has a private life and feels a concern for the public weal, can hardly fail to say. Unfortunately, like Professor Trilling's, these reflections upon science and culture are too abstract and general to be very enlightening. In the paragraphs that follow, I shall attempt to deal with this much-discussed theme in terms more concrete than those employed by Oppenheimer and Trilling, by Leavis, Snow and the Victorian initiators of the great debate. What is the function of literature, what its psychology, what the nature of literary language? And how do its function, psychology and language differ from the function, psychology and language of science? What, in the past, has been the relationship between literature and

6

science? What is it now? What might it be in the future? What would it be profitable, artistically speaking, for a twentieth-century man of letters to do about twentieth-century science? These are the questions I shall try to answer.

2

All our experiences are strictly private; but some experiences are less private than others. They are less private in the sense that, under similar conditions, most normal people will have similar experiences and, having had them, can be relied upon to interpret the spoken or written reports of such experiences in much the same way.

About the more private of our experiences no such statements can be made. For example, the visual, auditory and olfactory experiences of a group of people watching the burning of a house are likely to be similar. Similar, too, are the intellectual experiences of those members of the group who make the effort to think logically about the causes of this particular fire and, in the light of current knowledge, of combustion in general. In other words, sense impressions and the processes of rational thought are experiences whose privacy is not too extreme to make them unshareable. But now let us consider the emotional experiences of our fire-watchers. One member of the group may feel sexual excitement, another aesthetic pleasure, another horror, and yet others human sympathy or inhuman and malicious glee. Such experiences, it is obvious, are radically unlike one another. In this sense they are more private than sense experiences and the intellectual experiences of logical thought.

In the present context, science may be defined as a device for investigating, ordering and communicating the more public of human experiences. Less systematically, literature also deals with such public experiences. Its main concern, however, is with man's more private experiences, and with the interactions between the private worlds of sentient, self-conscious individuals and the public universes of 'objective reality', logic, social conventions and the accumulated information currently available.

3

*method
intent*

The man of science observes his own and the reports of other people's more public experiences; conceptualizes them in terms of some language, verbal or mathematical, common to the members of his cultural group; correlates these concepts in a logically coherent system; then looks for 'operational definitions' of his concepts in the world of nature, and tries to prove, by observation and experiment, that his logical conclusions correspond to certain aspects of events taking place 'out there'.

In his own way, the man of letters is also an observer, organizer and communicator of his own and other people's more public experiences of events taking place in the worlds of nature, culture and language. Viewed in a

*same raw
material*

certain way, such experiences constitute the raw material of many branches of science. They are also the raw material of much poetry, many dramas, novels and essays. But whereas the man of science does his best to ignore the worlds revealed by his own and other people's more private experiences, the man of letters never confines himself for long to what is merely public. With him, outer reality is

correspondence

constantly related to the inner world of private experience, shared logic modulates into unshareable feeling, *note need* wild individuality is forever breaking through the crust of

LITERATURE AND SCIENCE

cultural custom. Moreover the way in which the literary artist treats his subject matter is very different from the way in which the same subject matter is treated by the man of science. The scientist examines a number of parti- *deduction* cular cases, notes all similarities and uniformities and *from general* from these abstracts a generalization, in the light of which *to universal* (after it has been tested against the observed facts) all *one* other analogous cases may be understood and dealt with. His primary concern is not with the concreteness of some unique event, but the abstracted generalizations, in terms of which all events of a given class 'make sense'. The literary artist's approach to experience—even to experience of the more public kind—is very different. Repeatable experiments and the abstraction from experience of utilizable generalizations are not his business. His method *individual* is to concentrate upon some <u>individual case</u>, to look into *single* it so intently that <u>finally he is</u> enabled to look clean *leads to* <u>through it.</u> Every concrete particular, public or private, is *all cases* a window opening on to the universal. *King Lear, Hamlet, Macbeth*—three grisly anecdotes, about highly individualized human beings in exceptional situations. But through these records of unique and extremely improbable events occurring simultaneously in the worlds of private and public experience, Shakespeare saw, and miraculously made it possible for us to see, enlightening truth on every level from the theatrical to the cosmic, from the political to the sentimental and the physiological, from the all too familiarly human to the divinely unknowable.

The physical sciences started to make progress when investigators shifted their attention <u>from qualities to</u> ✓ <u>quantities</u>, from the appearances of things perceived as wholes to their fine structures; from the phenomena presented to consciousness by the senses to their invisible

9

beyond observation or experience

and intangible components, whose existence could only be inferred by analytical reason. The physical sciences are 'nomothetic'; they seek to establish explanatory laws, and these laws are most useful and enlightening when they deal with relationships between the invisibles and intangibles underlying appearances. These invisibles and intangibles cannot be described, for they are not objects of immediate experience; they are known only by inferences drawn from immediate experiences on the level of ordinary appearance. Literature is not 'nomothetic', but 'idiographic'; its concern is not with regularities and explanatory laws, but with descriptions of appearances and the *not seen* discerned qualities of objects perceived as wholes, with judgments, comparisons and discriminations, with 'inscapes' and essences, and finally with the *Istigkeit* of things, the Not-thought in thoughts, the timeless Suchness in an infinity of perpetual perishings and perpetual renewals.

metaphor also?

The world with which literature deals is the world into which human beings are born and live and finally die; the world in which they love and hate, in which they experience triumph and humiliation, hope and despair; the world of sufferings and enjoyments, of madness and common sense, of silliness, cunning and wisdom; the world of social pressures and individual impulses, of reason against passion, of instincts and conventions, of shared language and unshareable feeling and sensation; of innate differences and the rules, the roles, the solemn or absurd rituals imposed by the prevailing culture. Every human being is aware of this multifarious world and knows (rather confusedly in most cases) where he stands in relation to it. Moreover, and, by analogy with himself, he can guess where other people stand, what they feel and how they are likely to behave. As a private individual, the scientist inhabits the many-faceted world in which the rest of the human race does its living and dying. But as a professional chemist, say, a professional physicist or physiologist, he is the inhabitant of a radically different universe—not the *seeing world* universe of given appearances but the world of inferred fine structures, not the experienced world of unique events and diverse qualities, but the world of quantified regularities. Knowledge is power and, by a seeming paradox, it is through their knowledge of what happens in this unexperienced world of abstractions and inferences that scientists and technologists have acquired their enormous and growing power to control, direct and modify the world of manifold appearances in which human beings are privileged and condemned to live.

Every science has its own frame of reference. The data of physics are co-ordinated in one way, the data of ornithology (a science that is as yet a good deal more idiographic than nomothetic) are co-ordinated in another, *?* very different way. For Science in its totality, the ultimate goal is the creation of a monistic system in which—on the *search for unity* symbolic level and in terms of the inferred components of invisibly and intangibly fine structure—the world's enormous multiplicity is reduced to something like unity, and the endless succession of unique events of a great many different kinds gets tidied and simplified into a single rational order. Whether this goal will ever be reached remains to be seen. Meanwhile we have the various sciences, each with its own system of co-ordinating concepts, its own criterion of explanation.

The man of letters, when he is being most distinctively literary, accepts the uniqueness of events, accepts the diversity and manifoldness of the world, accepts the *diversity* radical incomprehensibility, on its own level, of raw, un-conceptualized existence and finally accepts the challenge which uniqueness, multifariousness and mystery fling in his face and, having accepted it, addresses himself to the paradoxical task of rendering the randomness and shape-lessness of individual existence in highly organized and meaningful works of art.

to make order from chaos

4

There exists in every language a rough and ready voca-bulary for the expression and communication of the individual's more private experiences. Anyone capable of speech can say, 'I'm frightened', or 'How pretty!', and those who hear the words will have a crude but, for most practical purposes, a sufficiently vivid idea of what is being talked about. Bad literature (bad, that is to say, on the private level—for, as quasi-science and in relation to man's more public experience, it may be quite good), bad literature hardly goes beyond the *how pretty*'s and *I'm frightened*'s of average everyday speech. In good literature —good, that is to say, on the private level—the blunt imprecisions of conventional language give place to subtler and more penetrating forms of expression. The ambition of the literary artist is to speak about the ineff-able, to communicate in words what words were never intended to convey. For all words are abstractions and stand for those aspects of a given class of experiences which are recognizably similar. The elements of experi-ence which are unique, aberrant, other-than-average, remain outside the pale of common language. But it is precisely these elements of man's more private experi-ences that the literary artist aspires to communicate. For this purpose common language is wholly inadequate.

Hemingway?

French? Symbolist

12

* seems a level very similar to science, to me, — the "invisible level" of p. 10.

LITERATURE AND SCIENCE

Every literary artist must therefore invent or borrow some
kind of uncommon language capable of expressing, at
least partially, those experiences which the vocabulary and
syntax of ordinary speech so manifestly fail to convey.
Donner un sens plus pur aux mots de la tribu—that is the
task confronting every serious writer; for it is only by an
unusual combination of purified words that our more
private experiences in all their subtlety, their many-
faceted richness, their unrepeatable uniqueness can be, in
some sort, re-created on the symbolic level and so made
public and communicable. And even so, even at the best,
how hopeless is the writer's task!

> They are the smallest pieces of the mind
> That pass the narrow organ of the voice;
> The great remain behind in that vast orb
> Of the apprehension, and are never born.

In paradise the saints experience a bliss *che non gustata non
s'intende mai.* And the same is true of the ecstasies and
pains of human beings here on earth. Untasted, they can
never be comprehended. In spite of 'all the pens that ever
poets held'—yes, and in spite of all the scientists' electron
microscopes, cyclotrons and computers—the rest is
silence, the rest is always silence.

5

As a medium of literary expression, common language is
inadequate. It is no less inadequate as a medium of scientific expression. Like the man of letters, the scientist finds
it necessary to 'give a purer sense to the words of the
tribe'. But the purity of scientific language is not the same
as the purity of literary language. The aim of the scientist

Malarmé = Huxley has a French notion of literature

is to say only one thing at a time, and to say it unam-
biguously and with the greatest possible clarity. To
achieve this, he simplifies and jargonizes. In other words,
he uses the vocabularly and syntax of common speech in
such a way that each phrase is susceptible of only one
interpretation; and when the vocabulary and syntax of
common speech are too imprecise for his purposes, he
invents a new technical language, or jargon, specifically
designed to express the limited meaning with which he
is professionally concerned. At its most perfectly pure,
scientific language ceases to be a matter of words and
turns into mathematics.

The literary artist purifies the language of the tribe in a
radically different way. The scientist's aim, as we have
seen, is to say one thing, and only one thing, at a time.
This, most emphatically, is not the aim of the literary
artist. Human life is lived simultaneously on many levels
and has many meanings. Literature is a device for report-
ing the multifarious facts and expressing their various
significances. When the literary artist undertakes to give a
purer sense to the words of his tribe, he does so with the
express purpose of creating a language capable of convey-
ing, not the single meaning of some particular science,
but the multiple significance of human experience, on its
most private as well as on its more public levels. He
purifies, not by simplifying and jargonizing, but by deep-
ening and extending, by enriching with allusive harmonics, with overtones of association and undertones of
sonorous magic.

What is a rose? A daffodil? A lily? One set of answers
to these questions may be given in the highly purified
languages of bio-chemistry, cytology and genetics. 'A
special form of ribonucleic acid (called messenger RNA)

14

carries the genetic message from the gene, which is located in the nucleus of the cell, to the surrounding cytoplasm, where many of the proteins are synthesized'. And so on in endless, fascinating detail. A rose is a rose is a rose, is RNA, DNA, polypeptide chains of amino acids. . . .

And here, on a considerably lower level of scientific purification, are the perfunctory botanical answers to our questions, provided by an encyclopaedia in its articles *Rose* and *Daffodil*. 'The carpels of the rose are concealed within the receptacular tube and only the stigmas as a rule project from its mouth. . . . By repeated radial and tangential branching a vast number of stamens are produced. . . . Under natural circumstances rose flowers do not secrete honey, the attraction for insects being provided by the colour and perfume and the abundance of pollen for food. . . . Conserve of dog rose is made from the ripe hips of *Rosa canina*. Its only use is in the manufacture of pills'. As for *Narcissus Pseudo-Narcissus*, 'Its flowers are large, yellow, scented and a little drooping, with a corolla deeply cleft into six lobes, and a central bell-shaped nectary, which is crisped at the margin. . . . The stamens are shorter than the cup, the anthers oblong and converging; the ovary is globose and has three furrows. . . . The bulbs are large and orbicular; they, as well as the flowers, are reputed to be emetic in properties.'

The primary interest of the literary artist is not in cells or genes or chemical compounds, not in the orbicularity of bulbs or the number of stamens, not even in the manufacture of pills or the concoction of herbal emetics. His concern is with his own and other people's more private experiences in relation to flowers and with the multiple meanings he finds in them. He is a man, and men must sweat for a living; so he considers the blessed lilies that toil not, neither do they spin. He is often depressed by too much thinking, or bored by too little; but, thank heaven, remembered daffodils flash upon that inward eye which is the bliss of solitude. 'A poet could not but be gay:' but alas, those brave flowers 'that come before the swallow dares, and take the winds of March with beauty' —how quickly they fade! The poet weeps to see them haste away so soon; weeps over time flying and approaching death and the loss of those he loves. *Et rose elle a vescu ce que vivent les roses, L'espace d'un matin.* And there is also the misguided idealist who weeps over *la metempsychose des lys en roses.* There is the unashamed sensualist who luxuriates in the thought of *la mousse où le bouton de rose brille.* There is the religious contemplative, alternately consoled and desolated, whose shrivelled heart, in a moment of dryness, 'goes quite under ground, as flowers depart', when their blossoming is over, to 'keep house with their mother root'—or, if you prefer the other kind of purified language, their orbicular bulb. And sometimes the lilies fester so that those rotting symbols of virginity come to smell worse than weeds. Sometimes, too, it is the rose that is sick; for the invisible worm 'has found out thy bed of crimson joy, and his secret love does thy life destroy'. But sometimes, miraculously, when the doors of perception have been cleansed, we find ourselves seeing a Heaven in a Wild Flower and holding Infinity in the palm of our hand. Sometimes, weary of time, the broad sunflower breaks out of the dark Tennysonian garden where it hangs so heavily over its own grave and comes to new apocalyptic life in that golden Eternity 'where the traveller's journey is done'. Very nice! comments the botanist, and proceeds to inform us that 'the genus *Helianthus* contains about fifty species, chiefly natives of North America, a few being found in Peru and Chile. In parts of England', he adds, 'hundreds of plants are grown for their seeds on sewage farms'.

6

The way in which scientists purify the words of their tribe requires no further illustration. From science to science technical jargons vary, of course, enormously. But the principles underlying jargonization, and the reasons for it, are always the same. So are the reasons for systematic simplification and the principle which decrees that every sentence in a scientific exposition shall say one thing, and one thing only, at a time.

In the works of literary art, as we have seen, common speech is treated to a very different kind of purification. Eschewing technical jargon, the man of letters takes the words of the tribe and, by a process of selection and novel arrangement, transforms them into another, purer language—a language in which it is possible to communicate unshareably private experiences, to give utterance to the ineffable, to express, directly or by implication, the diverse qualities and meanings of existence in the many universes—cosmic and cultural, inward and outward, given and symbolical—within which human beings are predestined, by their multiple amphibiousness, to live and move and have their bewildered being. Many, subtle, sometimes strange and extraordinary, are the ways in which the language of the tribe has been purified so as to make it capable of rendering human life in its collective fulness as well as its most intimate privacy, at its aesthetic, intellectual and spiritual heights as well as in its obscurest depths of instinct and physiology. Let us consider a few concrete examples of such linguistic purification.

7

I will begin on what may be called the macroscopic level. Here is a literary artist who wishes to express the multiple meanings of human existence in its fulness. How must he construct a narrative, say, or a drama, so as to convey these multiple meanings? One answer to this question is ✓ Shakespeare's *Troilus and Cressida*. Besides being a tragic drama, this extraordinary play is a vast repertory of life's multiple meanings. We are shown its meaning for the pathetically innocent and romantic Troilus; its meaning for Hector, the heroic idealist; for the ripe, intensely practical intelligence of Ulysses; for Helen and Cressida in their delicious universes of beauty and sexuality; for the two hulking mesomorphs, the idiot Ajax and the brighter but hardly less odious Achilles; and finally its meaning for Thersites, the man who can only hate, the universal debunker, the walking *memento mori*, for whom all flesh is excrement, syphilis and putrefaction.

✓ *War and Peace* provides another answer to our question. Inward and outward, personal and collective, concrete givenness and high abstraction—all the meanings of existence emerge as the novel's many characters live their lives and die their deaths, and as Tolstoy himself comments philosophically on the great historical movements in which they find themselves involved.

The possibility of shifting from objectivity to life's subjective meanings is built into the structure of almost every good novel. What a character does is described, now from the outside, now from within, now as others see the event and now as the protagonist feels it. Or con-

weakness already seen: in a novel we get the inner experience of someone by means of poêsis poiesis

sider the unshareableness of private experience. In a fictional narrative this is rendered by the juxtaposition of two parallel inwardnesses, or else of an inwardness and some simultaneous, but unconnected and irrelevant objectivity. One thinks, for example, of Emma Bovary after the love-making in the wood. 'Silence was everywhere; a sweetness seemed to come forth from the trees. She felt her heart, whose beating had begun again; she felt the blood coursing through her flesh like a stream of milk. Then, far away, beyond the wood, on the other hill, she *correlatives* heard a vague, long-drawn cry. In the silence she heard it mingling like music with the last pulsations of her *associational* nerves. Rodolphe, a cigar between his lips, was busy with his penknife, mending one of the two broken bridles'.

It should be remarked that this systematic shifting of attention from one order of experience to another is a literary device of rather recent invention. In *Moll Flanders*, for example, the narrative, although in the first person, is an account of events seen, in the main, from the outside. 'We had not sat long, but he got up, and stopping my very breath with kisses, threw me upon the bed again; but then being both well warmed, he went further with me than decency permits me to mention, nor had it been in my power to deny him in that moment, had he offered much more than he did.' About this kind of thing, there is an engaging artistic innocence. Very different is the calculated, one-track objectivity of *Candide*, from which private experience is deliberately and, so to say, flagrantly omitted for the express purpose of emphasizing the criminal stupidity, the absurd as well as hideous wickedness of human behaviour. Here is Voltaire's account of the *auto da fé* prescribed by the University of

Coimbra as a sure preventive of any repetition of the Lisbon earthquake.

> '*Ils marchèrent en procession ainsi vétus, et entendirent un sermon très pathétique, suivi d'une belle musique en faux-bourdon. Candide fut fessé en cadence pendant qu'on chantait; le Biscayen et les deux hommes qui n'avaient pas voulu manger le lard furent brûlés, et Pangloss fut pendu, quoique ce ne soit pas la coutume. Le même jour la terre trembla de nouveau avec un fracas épouvantable.*'

8

From purification of language on the level of structural anatomy we pass to purification on what may be called the cellular and molecular levels of the paragraph, sentence and phrase. It is mainly on these levels that the literary artist gives expression to the inexpressible and makes public the most private of experiences. Here, for example, is Emily Dickinson writing, in 'A Light Exists in Spring', about one of Nature's mysterious apocalypses and the sense of desolation that follows a moment of vision.

> A colour stands abroad
>> On solitary hills
> That science cannot overtake,
>> But human nature feels.

It is there, like a divine revelation; then abruptly, 'without the formula of sound, it passes, and we stay'.

> A quality of loss
>> Affecting our content,
> As trade had suddenly encroached
>> Upon a sacrament.

In this case a private experience has been rendered by the evocation of some of life's multiple meanings—trade and sacrament—in the world of collective action and conceptual thought. But there are, of course, many other ways in which the literary artist can talk about the ineffable.

> It is so quiet,
> The cicada's voice
> Penetrates
> The rocks.

In this *haiku* by Basho the experience recorded is of a unique event through which the Suchness of things, the divine Ground, as Meister Eckhart would call it, breaks out of eternity into time. To communicate this indescribable event, the Japanese poet has refined his utterance to the point where it seems about to turn into the *creux néant musicien* of a silence as absolute as that which filled the spaces between the rocks and by mysterious implication (and yet how indubitably!) imparted to the mindless repetition of insect noises a kind of absoluteness, a cosmic significance.

paradox again

At the other end of the world we find Andrew Marvell

> Annihilating all that's made
> To a green thought in a green shade.

Basho would have begun and ended there. In 'The Garden' green annihilation into green thought is only one incident among many. Marvell was working within a poetical tradition that concerned itself with a wider spectrum of life's multiple meanings than the writers of *haiku* had chosen as their domain.

no revelation in Huxley's literary language

9

At the opposite pole to the mode of expression by mysterious implication is the mode of direct expression by means of the *mot juste*. The tribe's language can be purified into expressiveness by the choice of the right noun, the perfect adjective, the supremely apt verb. For example, what does one feel when one hears good music? With two substantives and a pair of epithets, Milton provides an answer that is at once poetical and scientific in its purity: 'such sober certainty of waking bliss'. But the *mot juste* possesses only a limited usefulness. In most cases, the intimacies of our more private experience and the multiplicity of life's meanings cannot be translated directly with a one-to-one correspondence, into a single *mot juste*, or even into a single 'right' phrase or sentence. Here, to illustrate this point, are some of the words and phrases culled by Bishop Rovenius from the mystical literature of his time—the seventeenth century. *Inflaming transubstantiations; super-essential unions; absorbent enthusiasms; abyssal liquefactions; deific confrications; insupportable assaults; hypercelestial penetrations; spiritual shamelessness; meridian holocausts in a visceral and medullar penetrability.* Each of these strange locutions (my own favourite is 'deific confrications') is the product of a misguided effort on the part of some earnest and perhaps truly enlightened soul to purify the words of the tribe into a pseudo-scientific jargon of *mots justes* for classifying and communicating mystical experiences. But mystical experiences are at once too private and too enormous to be rendered by one-to-one translation into some unequivocally right and perfect phrase. If one is to talk about them at all, it must be by indirection—in terms, for example, of such paradoxical phrases as Crashaw's 'sweetly killing dart', or the *cauterio suave, regalada llaga* of St John of the Cross, or alternatively by mixing psychological description with metaphysics and theology. Thus Suso tells us that, for mystics, there is an immediate and completely private experience of light, and that, in this light, 'the mind dies, loses its individuality and is lost in the pure and simple unity'. And when the mystic says he loves God, precisely how does he love Him? 'As not-God', says Meister Eckhart, 'not-Spirit, not-Person, not-image, but as He is, a sheer, pure, absolute One, in whom we must continually sink from nothingness to nothingness'.

10

Hardly less enormous than the mystical union with God, and, although shared, hardly less unspeakably private, is the cognate experience of sexual union with a human partner. For the literary artist, the problem of communicating sexual experience is in some ways even more difficult than the problem of communicating mystical experience. What means of expression should he use? Scientific jargon and abstraction? Polite circumlocution? Spiritual analogies? Metaphysico-lyrical eloquence? Or the *mot juste*? Or, finally, the *gros mot*, the Saxon tetra-grammaton? These were questions, as I vividly remember, which I often discussed with Lawrence after a first reading of the manuscript of *Lady Chatterley*. For Lawrence, the scientific approach was, of course, completely out of the question. Almost equally out of the question were the elegant periphrases of eighteenth-century French literature. The exquisitely refined, the almost algebraic style of those drawing-room pornographers, who could write, without raising a blush on any lady's cheek, of little deaths, of wandering fingers and strayed lips, of pleasures knocking imperiously at every door, of frustrated lovers expiring on the threshold of the temple, seemed to him positively obscene. So did a sentimental spiritualization of 'The right true end of love'. Sex in the soul repelled him as strongly as did every kind of sex in the head, from the polysyllabically scientific to the prettily and periphrastically pornographic. So far as Lawrence was concerned, there was only one right way to communicate the right kind of sexual experience, and that was by means of a soaring lyrical eloquence, firmly anchored, however, to the most uncompromisingly explicit of four-letter words. In theory, this is obviously the best possible solution to our problem. In practice, unfortunately, and at this moment of history, within this particular culture, it has its drawbacks. Being still taboo, the Saxon tetra-grammata produce effects in the reader's mind out of all proportion to the frequency of their use. The Victorian novelists 'never talked obstetrics when the little stranger came' and never talked Krafft-Ebing during the honey-moon. Their books, in consequence, were unrealistic as 'criticisms of life'. But when contemporary novelists describe the various phases of the sexual cycle in words which we have been conditioned to regard as unprintable, the criticism of life becomes unrealistic through lop-sided over-emphasis. When four-letter words are used, every description of a sexual relationship carries a weight equivalent to the cube of that which its author intended it to carry. Five pages seem like a hundred and twenty-five, with the result that the balance of the book is upset and its composition distorted out of all recognition. Perhaps, after all, there was more to be said for eighteenth-century periphrases than Lawrence was ready to admit.

24

II

From the *gros mot* and the *mot juste* we pass to the in-directly expressive and essentially literary device of the metaphor. How many meanings emerge from such a phrase as 'those milk paps that through the window bars bore at men's eyes'! Or from 'the strongest oaths are straw to the fire i'the blood'! Individual instinct pitted against the repressive forces of society, the felt frenzies of desire against the conscience that makes cowards and reluctant good citizens of most of us, most of the time—these images of flame in the straw, of nippled gimlets behind a grating, evoke the everlasting conflict with in-comparable power. And meanwhile, rational or violently passionate, unregenerate or saved, human beings can never forget the all-pervading facts of their mortality and of time irreversibly flowing. In the purified language of literature metaphors of winged chariots, of fading flowers, of scythes and hour glasses, communicate the many meanings of existence in a world that is perpetually perishing. And here is the manifoldly expressive image with which Lamartine begins his greatest poem.

Ainsi toujours poussés vers de nouveaux rivages,
Dans la nuit éternelle emportés sans retour,
Ne pourrons nous jamais sur l'océan des âges
Jeter l'ancre un seul jour?

Ships give place to shuttles, and here is Henry Vaughan on the human condition.

Man is the shuttle to whose winding quest
And passage through these looms
God ordered motion, but ordained no rest.

The metaphor calls up a succession of ramifying after-images. What patterns do the incessantly hurrying shuttles weave? What is the quality of the cloth? And do the weavers *never* get a day off?

By means of metaphor we can talk about one thing in terms of something else and so, by indirection, express more of life's multiple meanings, subjective and objective, than can be expressed by straightforward speech. Literary allusion performs a very similar function:

> Oh, many a peer of England brews
> Livelier liquor than the Muse,
> And malt does more than Milton can
> To justify God's ways to man.

Theological argument or a change of body-chemistry, high philosophy or more vitamins, Calliope and Poly-hymnia or the inspirations of 'ale in a Saxon rumkin, such as will make Grimalkin prate'? Housman's four lines could be expanded into volumes of scientific evidence, medical case histories, metaphysical soliloquies and ethical disputations. And when an earlier poet speaks of god-like David who,

> wide as his command,
> Scattered his Maker's image through the land,

how richly comic, in the historical context of Charles II and his bedroom exploits, is this allusion to Genesis and the basic postulate of Christian anthropology! From Dryden's *Absalom and Achitophel* we pass to the work of a great contemporary poet. Literary allusion (along with direct quotation and parody) is the device for expressing life's multiple meanings chiefly employed by Mr T. S.

Eliot in *The Waste Land*. The human creature's equal and opposite capacities for the squalid and the sublime, for the subtlest refinement of sensibility and the most nauseating vulgarity, for an almost boundless intelligence and an almost bottomless stupidity, are rendered by the alternation of twentieth-century observations with allusions to, quotations from, or parodies of classical, medieval and modern literature.

12

Many other devices are employed by men of letters in their constant struggle to purify, and in purifying to enrich, the language of the tribe—devices to which, because they work on that obscure region lying between consciousness and physiology, have often been qualified as 'magical'. There is the magic, for example, of unfamiliarly beautiful syntax and sentence construction; the magic of names and words that, for some obscure reason, seem intrinsically significant; the magic of well-ordered rhythms, of harmonious combinations of consonants and vowels. One thinks of such exquisite treasures of syntax as 'Not to know me argues yourselves unknown', or *Tel qu'en Lui-même enfin l'éternité le change*. And at the other extreme of phrase-making one recalls the spell-like efficacity of such juxtaposed simplicities as 'Cover her face: mine eyes dazzle: she died young'; as 'I wak'd, she fled, and day brought back my night': as 'Princess Volupine arrived; they were together, and he fell'.

The supreme masters of syntactical magic are Milton and Mallarmé. Poetically speaking, *Paradise Lost* is *Syntax Regained*—regained and completely re-made. *Rature te vague littérature*, Mallarmé advised. Scratch out all words with a too specific reference to brute reality and

concentrate on the words themselves and their relationships within the phrase and sentence. Practising what he
preached, Mallarmé created, in the sonnets, a repertory of
syntactical marvels, unmatched in modern literature.

13

In certain contexts, intrinsically significant words and
names are supremely 'right'; but their rightness is quite
different from the rightness of the *mot juste*. The *mot juste*
is directly and almost scientifically meaningful; the intrinsically significant word or name is meaningful because
it has a beautiful sound, or because, for one reason or
another, it carries a reference to realms of experience
beyond itself. Thus, for Flaubert, '*La fille de Minos et de
Pasiphaé*' seemed, because of the sound of the names and,
no doubt, because of their ramifying mythological implications, 'the most beautiful line in all French literature,
a phrase of eternal and sublime loveliness'. From Homer
to Milton, every epic fairly rumbles with reverberating
names. Peor and Baalim; Argob and Basna; Abbana and
Pharphar, lucid streams. Elsewhere, and in lighter keys,
we find such enchantments as 'crossing the stripling
Thames at Bablock Hithe', or 'Amyntas now doth with
his Chloris sleep under a sycamore'. ('Sycamore' is an
intrinsically significant word that potentiates the idyllic
love-making of Chloris and her shepherd.) On a higher
level of intrinsic significance we find such Shakespearean
marvels as 'defunctive music', 'sole Arabian tree', 'multitudinous seas incarnadine'. And what about Milton's
'elephants endors'd with towers'? What about 'sleek
Panope' and 'that two-handed engine at the door'! And
here are three stanzas from Christopher Smart's *Nativity
of Our Lord*, in which the magics of harmonized sonorities

and intrinsically significant names have been powerfully combined.

> Where is this stupendous stranger!
>   Swains of Solyma, advise.
> Lead me to my Master's manger,
>   Shew me where my Saviour lies. . . .
>
> Boreas now no longer winters
>   On the desolated coast;
> Oaks no more are riv'n in splinters
>   By the whirlwind and his host.
>
> Spinks and ouzels sing sublimely,
>   'We too have a Saviour born.'
> Whiter blossoms burst untimely
>   On the blest Mosaic thorn.

The Nativity poem was evidently written during one of those happy intervals when Smart was neither too mad nor yet too sanely well-adjusted. Excess of adjustment inhibited his genius, too much madness resulted in such eccentricities as

> Let Ehud rejoice with Onocrotalus, whose braying is for the glory of God, because he makes the best music in his power.
>
> For I bless God that I am of the same seed as Ehud, Mutius Scaevola and Colonel Draper.

Betweenwhiles (fortunately for us) there were periods of premanic exaltation, during which, breaking out of the prison of eighteenth-century culture, Smart was able to give free rein to his extraordinary poetic gifts and yet retain complete intellectual control of what he was doing.

Sound, syntax, allusion, metaphor—in the *Nativity* and
A Song to David he revealed himself as a master of these
purificatory magics. And to all the rest he added the
ultimate magic—the magic of what may be called <u>verbal</u>
<u>recklessness</u>.

Some degree of verbal recklessness is characteristic of
good poetry. There are slightly reckless good poets, and
there are good poets who, at times, are extremely reckless.

> It moves us not.—Great God I'd rather be
> A Pagan suckled in a creed outworn;
> So might I, standing on this pleasant lea,
> Have glimpses that would make me less forlorn,
> Have sight of Proteus rising from the sea,
> Or hear old Triton blow his wreathed horn.

This is very good, but only moderately reckless. And now
here is the final stanza of Yeats's *Byzantium*.

> Astraddle on the dolphin's mire and blood,
> Spirit after spirit! The smithies break the flood,
> The golden smithies of the Emperor!
> Marbles of the dancing floor
> Break bitter furies of complexity
> Those images that yet
> Fresh images beget,
> That dolphin-torn, that gong-tormented sea.

In these lines verbal recklessness is splendidly uninhibited.
Yeats is purifying the words of the tribe by breaking their
traditional chains of dictionary-meaning, syntactical and
logical order. Of this private language of his he once
wrote

> I, being driven half insane
> Because of some green wing, gathered old mummy wheat

In the mad abstract dark, and ground it grain by grain
And after baked it slowly in an oven, but now
I bring full-flavoured wine out of a barrel found
Where seven Ephesian topers slept and never knew
When Alexander's empire passed, they slept so sound.

That barrel is the poet's pre-conscious mind—brought to
the surface by the power of verbal recklessness and in its
turn releasing the language of conventional speech into a
wilder, foolhardier intoxication.

14

Something like a theory of verbal recklessness was formulated by Rimbaud in his famous letter to Paul Demeny.
Dictionary definitions, fixed rules of syntax and grammar
—such things, he proclaimed, are only for the dead, for
fossils, in a word, for academicians. Every word is an
idea—by which he meant, I suppose, that when isolated
from the other words in relation to which it makes the
ordinary, accepted kind of sense, a word takes on a new
problematic, mysteriously magical significance. It becomes more than an idea; it becomes an *idée fixe*, a
haunting enigma. It is possible, as Tennyson discovered,
to talk oneself out of one's own familiar identity simply
by repeating the syllables of one's own name. And something analogous happens when one isolates a word, pores
over it, meditates upon it, treats it, not as an operational
element in some familiar kind of sentence, but as a thing-
in-itself, an autonomous pattern of sounds and meanings.
Out of word-ideas will be forged the future universal
language of poetry—a language 'resuming everything,
perfumes, sounds, colours, thought-stuff hooking on to
thought and tugging'. The poet must train himself to

French

become a seer, and the function of the poet-seer is 'to determine the precise amount of the unknown manifesting itself, during his life-time, in the universal soul'. Verbal recklessness opens unsuspected windows on to the unknown. By using liberated word-ideas in a reckless way, the poet can express, can evoke, can even create potentialities of experience hitherto unrecognized or perhaps non-existent, can discover aspects of the essential mystery of existence, which otherwise would never have emerged from that

> . . . multitudinous abyss
> Where secrecy remains in bliss,
> And wisdom hides her skill.

An ultimate and total verbal recklessness was advocated by the founding fathers of Dada. In an essay published in 1920, André Gide lucidly summarized the Dadaist philosophy. 'Every form has become a formula and distills an unspeakable boredom. Every common syntax is disgustingly insipid. The best attitude to the art of yesterday and in the face of accomplished masterpieces is not attempting to imitate them. The perfect is what does not need re-doing. . . . Already the edifice of our language is too undermined for anyone to recommend that thought should continue to take refuge in it. And before rebuilding it is essential to cast down what still seems solid, what makes a show of still standing. The words that the artifice of logic still lumps together must be separated, isolated. . . . Each vocable-island on the page must present steep contours. It will be placed here (or there, just as well) like a pure tone; and not far away will vibrate other pure tones, but without any interrelationships, so as to authorize no association of thoughts. Thus the word will be liberated from all its preceding meaning, at least, and from all evocation of the past'. Needless to say, it was psychologically and even physiologically impossible for the Dadaists to practise consistently what they preached. Do what they might, some kind of sense, some logical, syntactical, associational form of coherence kept breaking in. By the mere fact of being animals biologically committed to survival, of being human beings living in a certain place at a particular moment of history, they were compelled to be more consistent in thought and feeling, more grammatical and even more rational than, on their own principles, they ought to have been. As a literary movement, Dada failed. But even in its failure it rendered a service to poetry and to criticism by carrying to its logical, or rather to its illogical, conclusion the notion of verbal recklessness. In the scientist, verbal caution ranks among the highest of virtues. His words must have a one-to-one relationship with some specified class of data or sequence of ideas. By the rules of the scientific game he is forbidden to say more than one thing at a time, to attach more than one meaning to a given word, to stray outside the bounds of logical discourse, or to talk about his private experiences in relation to his work in the domains of public observation and public reasoning. Poets and, in general, men of letters are permitted, indeed are commanded, by the rules of *their* game, to do all the things that scientists are not allowed to do. There are occasions, obviously, when it is right for them to be verbally prudent; but there are other occasions when verbal imprudence, carried to a pitch if necessary, of the most extravagant foolhardiness, becomes an artistic duty, a kind of categorical imperative.

The ability to have poetical impressions is common. The ability to give poetical *ex*pression to poetical *im*pressions is very rare. Most of us can feel in a Keatsian way, but almost none of us can write in a Keatsian way. Among other things, a poem or, in general, any work of literary art, is a device for inducing in the reader impressions of the same kind as those which served as raw materials for the finished product. It may even happen that the impressions induced in the reader's mind are of a higher order of 'poeticalness' than those from which the writer set out. At its most magical, the purified language of literature can evoke experiences comparable to the pre-mystical or fully mystical apocalypses of pure receptivity on the non-verbal level. The Not-Thought that is in thoughts, the *Istigkeit* or Essential Suchness of the world may be discovered in our experiences of a poem about a flower in the crannied wall as well as in our experience (if the doors of perception are cleansed) of the flower itself. With such fragments of apocalyptic art we may, in Mr Eliot's words, shore up our ruins, may (as Matthew Arnold phrased it) 'prop in these bad days our mind'. And the shoring and propping will be almost as effective, perhaps for some people quite as effective, as the support provided by yellow bees in the ivy bloom or a host of golden daffodils. Change the wording of a work of literary art, and straightway all its apocalyptic quality, all its mysterious ability to prop minds and shore up ruins vanish into thin air. Change the wording of a scientific paper and, so long as clarity is preserved, no loss has been suffered. The purified language of science is instrumental, a device for making public experiences understandable by

fitting them into an existing frame of reference, or into a
new frame of reference that can take its place among the
old. The purified language of literary art is not the means
to something else; it is an end in itself, a thing of intrinsic
significance and beauty, a magical object endowed, like
Grimm's *Tischlein* or Aladdin's lamp, with mysterious
powers. Being merely instrumental, a scientific exposition
can be re-organized and re-phrased in dozens of different
ways, each of which will be perfectly satisfactory. And
when new facts have made it obsolete, these expositions
will go the way of all earlier scientific writings and be
forgotten. The fate of a work of literary art is very
different. Good art survives. Chaucer was not made
obsolete by Shakespeare. Intrinsic beauty and significance
are long-lived; instrumental information and instrumental
explanations within some scientific frame of reference are
ephemeral. But the sum and succession of these ephemeral
productions is a monument more enduring than bronze—
a dynamic monument, a Great Pyramid perpetually on
the move and growing larger all the time. This formid-
able structure is the totality of advancing science and
technology. And let us not forget that 'a heart that
watches and receives'—watches Nature, watches Art, and
thankfully receives whatever graces of insight they may
bestow, whatever props they may offer—would soon
come to a miserably bad end if it were not associated with
a brain that turns raw experience into logically connected
concepts, and with hands that, guided by these concepts,
make novel experiments and practise familiar skills. Man
cannot live by contemplative receptivity and artistic
creation alone. As well as every word proceeding
from the mouth of God, he needs science and technology.

35

Public and private. Objective and subjective. The world
of concepts and the multitudinous abyss of immediate
experience. The simplified, jargonized purity of scientific
discourse and the magical, many-meaninged purity of
literature. In this second half of the twentieth century,
how should the Two Cultures of Snow's dichotomy be
related?

2 Cultures

What the relationship between them ought *not* to be is
obvious. It ought not, for example, to be a relationship of
the kind described by Darwin in his autobiography. As a
youth, Darwin had taken pleasure in the poetry of Milton
and Wordsworth; but in his later twenties he began to be
afflicted by 'a curious and lamentable loss of the higher
aesthetic tastes'. Milton and Wordsworth now seemed to
him intolerably silly and, when he tried to re-read Shakespeare, he experienced a boredom so intense that it made
him feel physically sick.

Some of the poets have been as extreme in their literary
one-sidedness as was Darwin in his compulsive addiction
to selected facts and the purified simplicities of scientific
exposition. For example, Blake could never forgive the
scientists for having analysed the divine mystery of
immediate experience into its merely physical and measur-
able elements—'the atoms of Democritus and Newton's
Particles of light'. Animated by the same anti-scientific
spirit, Keats drank destruction to the man who had explained the rainbow and so robbed it of its poetry.

But one can be a practising scientist without sacrificing
one's love or one's understanding of literature. Darwin's
younger contemporary and champion, T. H. Huxley, has
left it on record that 'I have never met with any branch of

human knowledge which I have found unattractive—
which it would not have been pleasant to me to follow as
far as I could go; and I have yet to meet with any form of
art in which it has not been possible for me to take as
acute a pleasure as, I believe, it is possible for men to take'.

And from the other side of the spiritual Iron Curtain
separating the Two Cultures comes the voice of William
Wordsworth. Like Keats, Wordsworth was a passionate
lover of rainbows ('My heart leaps up when I behold a
rainbow in the sky'); and like Blake, he prized imagination, impulses from vernal woods and the 'wise passive-
ness' of intuition more highly than 'analytic industry' and
the scientist's 'single vision' of the world. But this did
not prevent him from admiring Sir Isaac, whose statue
('with his prism and silent face') was, for the young poet,

> The marble index of a mind for ever
> Voyaging through strange seas of thought, alone.

Alone. Despite the fact that his concern is with those less
private experiences which are roughly the same in all
human beings, the scientist, in Wordsworth's view, is
essentially a solitary figure, self-condemned to exile from
common humanity. The truth he seeks is not the intimate,
felt truth of our subjective life. It is truth from the outside, organized into a system of merely rational explanation, by a process of abstraction and hypothesis. The man
of science is radically unlike the poet who, 'singing a song
in which all human beings join with him, rejoices in the
presence of truth as our visible friend and hourly com-
panion'. The poet, Worsdworth continues, 'is the rock of
defence for human nature; an upholder and preserver,
carrying everywhere with him relationship and love. In
spite of difference of soil and climate, of language and

manners, of laws and customs; in spite of things silently gone out of mind, and things violently destroyed, the Poet binds together by passion and knowledge the vast empire of human society, as it is spread over the whole earth and over all time. . . . Poetry is the first and last of all knowledge; it is as immortal as the heart of man. . . . If the labours of Men of science should ever create any material revolution, direct or indirect, in our condition, and in the impressions which we habitually receive, the Poet will sleep then no more than at present; he will be ready to follow the steps of the Men of science, not only in those general indirect effects, but he will be at his side, carrying sensations into the midst of the objects of science itself. The remotest discoveries of the Chemist, the Botanist, or Mineralogist, will be as proper objects of the Poet's art as any upon which it can be employed, if the time should ever come when these things shall be familiar to us, and the relations under which they are contemplated by the followers of these respective sciences shall be manifestly and palpably material to us as enjoying and suffering beings. If the time should ever come when what is now called science, thus familiarized to men, shall be ready to put on, as it were, a form of flesh and blood, the Poet will lend his divine spirit to aid the transfiguration, and will welcome the Being thus produced as a dear and genuine inmate of the household of man'.

'*If* the time should ever come. . . .' In that *if* resides our whole problem. *If* all of us were as passionately interested in, say, the genetics of earthworms or the atomic hypothesis, as we are in our friendships, our arthritis or our sex life, *then*, obviously, there would be only one culture, not two. Poets would write lyrics indifferently about Nucleic Acid and their coy mistresses, about Quantum Mechanics

and the death of children; and research workers would
find it pleasant and even profitable to read these lyrics.
But the hypotheses of physics and the data of genetics and
bio-chemistry seem important only to a minority. Most
people are little interested in science as dispassionate
observation, still less interested in science as a rational
system of explanatory concepts. And even in the field of
applied science, of science as it is embodied in technology,
their concern is only with such matters as affect them
personally. 'If the labours of Men of science should ever
create any material revolution. . . .' Even in Wordsworth's
time these labours had begun to create a very considerable
material revolution. Today that revolution is chronic and
galloping.

A material revolution is never merely material. It
begets parallel revolutions in many other realms—social,
political and economic revolutions, revolutions in philosophical and religious thought, revolutions in ways of life
and modes of individual behaviour. It is with these
consequences of advancing technology, not with technology as a set of practical receipts, technology as the
application of scientific theories, that most human beings
are concerned.

17

As a class, men of letters have reacted to science and technology in much the same way as the majority of their less
talented fellows. They have not been greatly interested in
science as a set of logically coherent hypotheses validated
operationally by experiment and dispassionate observation. And in the field of applied science their concern has
been mainly with the social and psychological consequences of advancing technology, very little with its

working or its underlying theories. In the whole corpus of classical literature there is only one poem that celebrates a labour-saving machine—Antipater's brief piece in the Greek Anthology about the water-driven mill that had freed the slave women from the daily drudgery of grinding wheat or barley into flour. And in modern times Diderot is the only considerable writer who took the trouble to acquaint himself with the technology of his time, and who used his talents in order to communicate his knowledge. Most men of letters, when they write about technology, do so only as enjoying and suffering beings, not as accurate observers interested in the embodied logic of machinery. In the golden age of steam engines Tennyson seems to have believed that trains ran, not on rails, but in 'ringing grooves'. Ruskin objected to locomotives because their manufacturers had not disguised them as fire-breathing dragons. Victor Hugo wrote enthusiastically about the *Great Eastern*—but in words so wildly rhetorical that no concrete ideas about the size, appearance and capacities of Brunel's famous ship can be derived from them. Gabriele d'Annunzio's lyrical response to the internal combustion engines of aeroplanes and racing cars are hardly more realistic than Victor Hugo's dithyrambs about steamers and railway engines. At least in their published works, these writers exhibited very little interest in the scientific theories underlying the technological achievements of their time, even less interest in the methods by which these theories were applied to the solution of practical problems.

18

It is worth remarking in this context that, until very recent times, the creators of Utopias have been abysmally

because not seen as valid - so
what? (Reveals a protestant bias)

LITERATURE AND SCIENCE

uninventive in the fields of pure and applied science. A
lively scientific and technological imagination is a by-
product of rapidly advancing science and technology. In
an age of primitive science and rudimentary technology,
even the most brilliantly original minds are incapable of
imagining a state of affairs radically unlike that with
which they are familiar. Leonardo made designs for tanks
and air-conditioning machines; but he was unable to
imagine any sources of power different from those available at the beginning of the sixteenth century—the power
developed by human and animal muscles, and the power
developed by wind and falling water. The 'projectors' of
the seventeenth century talked grandiosely about mech-
anized agriculture; but their giant combines were to be
driven by windmills—consequently could never work.
From the days of Icarus until 1783, the problem of flying
was thought about in terms of artificial wings flapped by
the movements of human arms and legs. After Mont-
golfier, Utopian phantasy was able to conjure up visions
of manned gas bags with masts and sails. A few years
later the imaginary dirigibles were provided with recipro-
cating steam engines and aerial paddle wheels. In the
eighteen-sixties Jules Verne's more daring flights of fancy
were made possible by another half-century of accelerating scientific and technological progress. In the hundred
years that have passed since the inventor of Science
Fiction embarked on his career, science and technology
have made advances of which it was impossible for the
author of *From the Earth to the Moon* even to dream.
Rooted as they are in the facts of contemporary life, the
phantasies of even a second-rate writer of modern Science
Fiction are incomparably richer, bolder and stranger than
the Utopian or Millennial imaginings of the past.

From this brief excursion into the history of scientific fancy I pass to scientific facts and theories, and the ways in which at successive periods of history, these facts and theories have influenced literary artists, especially the poets.

Greece had a long tradition of utilitarian-didactic and scientifico-philosophic poetry. Hesiod's *Works and Days* contains, among other matters, a brief metrical treatise on agriculture and sheep-herding. Scientific and philosophical poetry was the product of a later age than Hesiod's. Unfortunately only a few fragments survive of the poem in which Parmenides expounded his theories about the One and the Many, contrasting conceptual 'truth' with merely probable 'opinions' about observed phenomena. And the same fate befell the splendid work in which Empedocles obscurely foreshadowed a theory of elementary particles, a theory of random variations and combinations resulting in something like the survival of the fittest, and a theory of the dependence of mental upon bodily states, with its curious corollary that ethics is largely a matter of correct diet. Passing from Greek to Latin literature, we find two perfectly preserved masterpieces, the *De Rerum Natura* of Lucretius and Virgil's *Georgics*—the first a scientific and philosophical work on the grandest scale, the second a set of versified essays, miraculously poetical, on the charms of country living and the techniques of agriculture. As science became more systematic, didactic poetry gave place to expository prose. In recent European literature the full-blown didactic poem, on themes of pure or applied science, becomes an anomaly and an anachronism, attractive only to a special breed of second-rate poets. The *Georgics* are succeeded, in modern times, by John Phillips's *Cyder*, Dyer's *Fleece*, the Abbé Delille's *Les Jardins*. And in place of *De Rerum Natura* we get Tiedge's dismal *Urania* and the elegant absurdities of Erasmus Darwin. In recent centuries no poet of the first rank has even tried to do what Lucretius and Empedocles did. Where scientific theory and scientific information have entered poetry, it has been incidentally. But the problem of the right relationship between literature and science presents itself even when a poet's references to scientific facts and theories are of the most casual nature. Consider, for example, these two stanzas, the first from John Donne's *A Valediction*, the second from *The Extasie* by the same poet.

[handwritten annotations in margin: "split / came very / early"]

> Moving of th'earth brings harms and fears;
>> Men reckon what it did and meant;
> But trepidation of the spheres,
>> Though greater far, is innocent.

And

> As our blood labours to beget
>> Spirits, as like souls as it can,
> Because such fingers need to knit
>> That subtle knot which makes us man . . .

Donne was well informed about the science of his day and, in these learned similes, he made a most ingenious use of his knowledge to illustrate his private experience of parting and of nuptial consummation. For readers brought up on the natural philosophy of the Schoolmen, his scientific allusions must have seemed brilliantly illuminating. But ours is the universe, not of Ptolemy and Galen, but of Palomar and Jodrell Bank, of bio-chemistry

43

and the EEG. If we still read Donne, it is because, in his own strange way, he gave a purer sense to the words of the tribe and because, in those purified words, he movingly expressed certain private experiences very like our own. We do not read him because he was knowledgeable in pre-Copernican astronomy and pre-Harveian physiology. The trepidation of the spheres, the animal and vital spirits—these things do not interest us. Why should they? We know that spheres and spirits don't exist and, unless we happen to be well-read in the history of obsolete science, we have no idea why the spheres trepidated or how the blood-begotten spirits knitted their subtle knot.

Similar difficulties confront the modern student of Dante. Why do we continue to read the *Divine Comedy*? Because its author saw clearly, felt intensely and was supremely, almost miraculously, a purifier of words. But as well as a poet, Dante was a scholar, a man of profound learning, interested in all the problems of philosophy and science as they were posed, discussed and (so the Schoolmen bumptiously believed) definitively solved by the metaphysicians and theologians of his time. Reading the *Divine Comedy*, the modern student is confronted by passages which, because they refer, in a marvellous kind of poetic shorthand, to the facts and theories of medieval science, are incomprehensible. What, for example, is he to make of

> *il settentrion del primo cielo*
> *che nè occaso mai seppe nè orto*
> *nè d'altra nebbia che di colpa velo,*
>
> *e che faceva lì ciascuno accorto*
> *di suo dover, come il piu basso face*
> *qual timon gira per venire a porto?*

44

seems a good reason to leave science out of poetry, to me.

Without the assistance of an editor and an apparatus of scholarly notes, the twentieth-century reader does not and cannot know what Dante is talking about.

In so far as he concerns himself with his own and other people's more private experiences, 'the Poet', as Wordsworth says, 'binds together by passion and knowledge the vast empire of human society, as it appears over the whole earth and over all time'. But when they concerned themselves with the other kind of knowledge—knowledge of external facts correlated within a logically coherent system of concepts—even the greatest poets completely failed to bind the empire of human society 'over all time'. After a few centuries, or a few generations, their scientific similes and illustrations, once so vivid, so penetratingly topical, lost their point and became at last completely incomprehensible. And the more precise the references to obsolete science, the more grotesque will they seem to readers of a later and, scientifically speaking, more enlightened age. Dante's cosmology is extremely precise. It is this precision which makes his incidental references to science so obscure and which invests his picture of the universe (that stuffy, all-too-human cosmos of the Middle Ages, in which everything in Nature is merely an illustration of some notion of Aristotle's, some phrase in the Bible) with its curious and rather distasteful quality of sublime absurdity.

For the readers of a later age, the scientific and theological imprecisions of Shakespeare are preferable to the more exact expressions of Dante or Donne.

> Sit, Jessica. Look how the floor of heaven
> Is thick inlaid with patens of bright gold.
> There's not the smallest orb which thou behold'st

But in his motion like an angel sings,
Still quiring to the young-eyed cherubins;
Such harmony is in immortal souls,
But whilst this muddy vesture of decay
Doth grossly close it in, we cannot hear it.

The Ptolemaic system, the Pythagorean music of the spheres, Aristotle's *De Coelo*, Jewish and Christian angelology—the whole elaborate apparatus of classical and medieval science, philosophy and theology is here taken for granted. But fortunately Shakespeare refrains from going into details. There are none of Donne's trepidations, none of Dante's Septentrions of the First Heaven. The imagery is precise on the poetical, not on the scientific level. It is only implicitly that Shakespeare tells us about his astronomical and philosophical theories. Explicitly he is talking about two lovers and their reactions to a starlit summer night.

From the sixteenth we jump to the nineteenth century, and an eloquent piece of free verse by Walt Whitman, a sonnet by Gerard Manley Hopkins.

When I heard the learn'd astronomer,
When the proofs, the figures, were ranged in columns
    before me,
When I was shown the charts and diagrams, to add,
    divide, and measure them,
When I sitting heard the astronomer where he lectured
    with much applause in the lecture-room,
How soon unaccountable I became tired and sick,
Till rising and gliding out I wandered off by myself,
In the mystical moist night air, and from time to time,
Looked up in perfect silence at the stars.

Grau, theurer Freund, ist alle Theorie, Und gruen des Lebens goldner Baum. For some people the contemplation of scientific theories is an experience hardly less golden than the experience of being in love or looking at a sunset. Whitman was not one of them. As an enjoying and suffering being, he was left cold by the facts and hypotheses of astronomy; he preferred silence and the stars. For a poet, this is an entirely legitimate preference. Not at all legitimate, it seems to me, is Hopkins's reaction to starlight in terms of an obsolete astronomy with animistic overtones.

> Look at the stars! Look, look up at the skies!
> O look at all the fire-folk, sitting in the air!
> The bright boroughs, the circle-citadels there!

This, surely, is to make the worst of both worlds—theory and life, concepts and immediate experience. In these opening lines of an otherwise admirable sonnet, Hopkins, the incomparable renderer in purified words of a sensibility that could capture the essences, the characteristic 'inscapes' of unique events, lapses into the rhetoric of scientific theory—of a theory, moreover, that, at the time he wrote, had been untenable for at least two hundred years. Those 'fire-folk sitting in the air', those 'bright boroughs' and 'circle citadels' might have served the 'learn'd astronomer' of the sixteenth century as explanatory concepts. Under the pen of a Victorian poet, even of a Victorian poet whose favourite philosopher was Duns Scotus, they are simply inadmissible.

20

Dante's Septentrions of the First Heaven, Donne's trepidations and blood-begotten spirits—for the modern reader,

such references to an obsolete science are mere obstacles
to understanding and sympathy. Does this mean that the
modern man of letters should take his cue from Whitman
—paying the tribute that literature owes to science by
attending the learn'd astronomer's lecture, only to re-
assert literature's complete autonomy by sneaking out,
before the end, and looking up in perfect silence at the
stars? My own belief is that he should try to make the best
of all the worlds in which, willy-nilly, he has to live—the
world of stars and the world of astro-physics, the world
of crowded halls and the world of silence, the worlds of
grey theory, green life and many-coloured poetry. But
Donne and Dante are there to demonstrate that, in a
matter of centuries or even of years, an allusion to science
may become incomprehensible. What of that? Even when
he says he is writing for posterity, the man of letters is in
fact addressing a contemporary audience. The audience
may consist, for the moment, only of himself; but even a
soliloquy is not immediately addressed to posterity. Moreover, even if one does write for posterity, the chances that
posterity will read what one has written are pretty slim.
And there is another point to remember. It is unlikely
that present-day science will become as totally obsolete as
the science of an earlier day, whose towering theories
were built upon inadequate foundations and whose explanatory concepts had never been operationally defined
and validated. Between Dante's universe and the universe
of modern astronomy there is a difference in kind; but
between the universe of modern astronomy and the
universe of astronomy two or three centuries from now
there will, in all probability, be a difference only in degree
and in detail. Our ancestors' references to trepidations and
the first heaven are now incomprehensible. But *our* refer-

48

ences to extra-galactic nebulae and supernovae will prob- *a faith statement*
ably make quite good sense even to our great-great-
grandchildren. Twentieth-century science is operationally
validated and so is unlikely to become as completely
obsolete as the science of the past. And, even if it should
become so obsolete that our descendants cannot understand our scientific allusions, what matter? Our descendants will not be reading us anyhow—so why worry? Why
not get on with the job—the surely important and
necessary job—of breaching the spiritual Iron Curtain?

21

Before embarking on speculations about what ought to be
done, or what might be done by men of letters in a
scientific age, let us consider what in fact has been done.
How have modern poets reacted to the great scientific
discoveries of our century, to its fantastic inventions, to
its vast structures of logically coherent, pragmatically useful, and yet wildly improbable concepts? To what extent
has the subject matter of poetry, or even its casual images
and illustrations, been affected by the extraordinary
things that have been happening, for the last two or three
generations, in the fields of scientific thought, investiga-
tion and experiment, of technological invention and
application? These are questions which I posed, more
than forty years ago, in an essay on the subject matter of
poetry; and this is how, more than forty years ago, I
answered them.

'The propagandists would have us believe that the
subject matter of contemporary poetry is new and start-
ling, that modern poets are doing something which has
not been done before. "Most of the poets represented in
these pages", writes Mr Louis Untermeyer in his *Anthology*

of Modern American Poetry, "have found a fresh and vigorous material in a world of honest and hard reality. They respond to the spirit of their times; not only have their views changed, their vision has been widened to include things unknown to the poets of yesterday. They have learned to distinguish real beauty from mere prettiness, to wring loveliness out of squalor, to find wonder in neglected places, to search for hidden truths even in the dark caves of the unconscious". Translated into practice, this means that contemporary poets can now write, in the words of Mr Carl Sandburg, of the "burr and boom of the blast fires", of "wops and bohunks". It means, in fact, that they are at liberty to do what Homer did—to write freely about the immediately moving facts of everyday life. Where Homer wrote about horses and the tamers of horses, our contemporaries write of trains, automobiles and the various species of wops and bohunks who control the horsepower. That is all. Much too much stress has been laid on the newness of the new poetry; its newness is simply a return from the jewelled exquisiteness of the eighteen-nineties to the facts and feelings of ordinary life. There is nothing intrinsically novel or surprising in the introduction into poetry of machinery and industrialism, of labour unrest and depth psychology; these things belong to us, they affect us daily as enjoying and suffering beings; they are a part of our lives, just as the kings and warriors, the horses, the chariots, the picturesque mythology, were part of Homer's life. The subject-matter of the new poetry remains the same as that of the old. The old boundaries have not been extended. There would be a real novelty in it if it had worked out a satisfactory method for dealing with scientific abstractions. It has not'.

In the forty years that have passed since these words were written has there been any significant change in the poetical situation? Several greatly gifted writers have purified and enriched the language of English and American poetry, have created and developed new rhythms, new metrical forms, new magics of syntax, sound and verbal recklessness. But the domain of poetry has not been notably enlarged. 'T. S. Eliot must be saluted', writes Mr Kenneth Allott, 'for his extension of the field of subject-matter available for poetic treatment. Christianity, the modern industrial city and the background of European history are found a place in his poetry, as MacNeice has remarked, and wit, irony and satire are weapons at his command'. But one may also remark, without the aid of Mr MacNeice, that Christianity has for some time been the subject-matter of quite a lot of poems, that modern industrial cities could not have been written about in the days before they existed and that European history was copiously treated by Victor Hugo, for example, and Robert Browning. As for wit, irony and satire—these can hardly be regarded as novelties. Eliot is a great poet because he purified the words of the tribe in novel, beautiful and many-meaninged ways, not because he extended the field of subject-matter available to poetic treatment: he didn't. And this is true of most of his poetical successors. From their writings you would be hard put to it to infer the simple historical fact that they are the contemporaries of Einstein and Heisenberg, of computers, electron microscopes and the discovery of the molecular basis of heredity, of Operationalism, Diamat and Emergent Evolution. Scientific facts and theories, the logical-empirical philosophy of science and the more comprehensive philosophies of man and nature which may legitimately be drawn from science as it is related to private experience in a particular social and historical context—these have as yet hardly found their way into modern poetry. Thus, the historians of modern English and American literature speak of the nineteen-twenties as 'being concerned in poetry with culture and the preservation of tradition'—Snow's non-scientific culture, of course, and the Judaeo-Christian and Graeco-Roman traditions associated with that culture. The poets of the nineteen-thirties displayed (in the jargon of modern criticism) a 'marked insistence on social reference'. So did the author of *Piers Plowman*, so did Shelley in *The Mask of Anarchy*. There is no enlargement of the poetic domain, merely the re-occupancy of a neglected province. The forties witnessed a reaction from 'social reference' to 'self-unravelling', Christianity and neo-romanticism. In the fifties we find a bit of everything—everything, that is to say, except an insistence on the kind of scientific reference that one might have expected to be a feature of poetic writing in a time of enormous progress in pure and applied science. In the forty years which have elapsed since I first commented on the old subject-matter of the new poetry, astonishingly few poems with a scientific reference have been written. Some elegant pieces of Neo-Metaphysical poetry by William Empson, Kenneth Rexroth's reflective lyric, 'Lyell's Hypothesis Again'—these are the only examples that come, offhand, to my mind. There must, of course, be others—but not many of them, I am sure. Of the better poems written since 1921, the great majority do not so much as hint at the most important fact of contemporary history—the accelerating progress of science and technology. In so far as they affect the social, economic and political situation in which individuals find themselves, some of the consequences of progressive science receive attention from the poets; but science as a growing corpus of information, science as a system of concepts operationally defined, even science as a necessary element in the formulation of a tenable philosophy of nature and man, science in a word as science, is hardly even mentioned. More exclusively even than their predecessors in earlier centuries, modern poets concern themselves with their own and other people's more private experiences as these are evoked by nature, by social pressures, by theological and political notions, by love and pain and bliss, by bereavement and the prospect of death.

22

That the poetry of this most scientific of centuries should be, on the whole, less concerned with science than was the poetry of times in which science was relatively unimportant is a paradox that requires to be elucidated and explained. To begin with, the very fact that this is an age of science has relieved poetry of the need to have much direct and detailed scientific reference. Progress in science has begotten progress in the popularization of science. Every year witnesses the publication of literally scores of surveys and bird's eye views of all the sciences, of summaries of recent advances, digests of current modes of thinking. 'Popular Science' is a new art form, partaking simultaneously of the text book and the *reportage*, the philosophical essay and the sociological forecast. There is now no necessity for science to enter poetry except by philosophic implication, as one of the indispensable constituents in a tenable world-view, or else by way of meaningful illustration or expressive metaphor. That so few contemporary poets should go in for scientific reference on a large scale or in detail is not surprising. What is surprising is that there are not more of them to whom, as to Tennyson, for example, and Laforgue, science is a personal-metaphysical concern, as well as a concern on the political and cultural levels of public experience.

In the good old days, we are often told, science was a great deal simpler than it is at present. Even a poet could understand the Darwinian hypothesis in its primitive form —could understand and rejoice, if he were a free-thinker, over its anti-theological implications or, if he were an orthodox Christian, react indignantly or with nostalgic tears to what *The Origin of Species* had done to Noah's Ark and the first chapter of *Genesis*. Today the picture, once so beautifully clear, has had to incorporate into itself all the complexities of modern genetics, modern bio-chemistry, even modern bio-sociology. Science has become an affair of specialists. Incapable any longer of understanding what it is all about, the man of letters, we are told, has no choice but to ignore contemporary science altogether.

And yet, for all the labyrinths within labyrinths revealed, as scientific analysis probes ever deeper into the fine structure of the world, the great philosophical problems remain—although seen in a different light—what they have always been: enormous, glaring, inescapable. Nature is just as red in tooth and claw as it was in Victorian times—and humanity, alas, far redder. We know a great deal more than Tennyson's contemporaries did about the 'flaring atom streams, running along the illimitable inane'—and much less than some of them thought they knew about a Creator within or beyond the atom stream. Is ours the only intelligence in an otherwise mindless infinity? We have better reasons than the Victorians had for believing that there are other habitable planets revolving about distant suns—thousands of millions of them in the single cosmic parish of our own galaxy. Tennyson was sure that the dark little worlds running round those other suns 'are worlds of woe like our own'. We have no good reason for disagreeing. *Woe* rhymes with *know*, suffering is a resultant of embodied awareness, a consequence of being a sentient individual. We are back again at the heart of the problem of mind. Where does consciousness fit into the cosmic picture? How did the illimitable inane get on without the perceiving, feeling and thinking inhabitants of this and all the other dark little worlds of woe, bliss, love, and frustration —not to mention poetry and science? And how will it get on when we are all gone?

> *Et ces couchants seront tout solitaires,*
> *Tout quotidiens et tout supre-Véda,*
> *Tout aussi vrais que si je n'étais pas,*
> > *Tout à leur affaire.*
>
> *Ah! ils seront tout aussi quotidiens*
> *Qu'au temps où la planète à la dérive*
> *En ses langes de vapeur primitive*
> > *Ne savait rien d'rien.*
>
> *Ils seront tout aussi à leur affaire*
> *Quand je ne viendrai plus crier bravo!*
> *Aux assortiments de mourants joyaux*
> > *De leur éventaire.*
>
> *Qu'aux jours où certain bohème filon*
> *Du commun néant n'avait pas encore*
> *Pris un acces d'existence pécore*
> > *Sous mon pauvre nom.*

What is and what ought to be, human aspiration and natural phenomena—the problems that were raised by science three and four generations ago are still with us, and the philosophers of science are still trying to work out acceptable solutions. But the poets, oddly enough, don't seem to be interested.

23

From the poets we now pass to the dramatists. What is the extent of *their* interest in science?

The function of drama is to arouse and finally allay the most violent emotions, and its basic theme is conflict—conflict between passionate individuals or conflict between one passionate individual and the categorical imperatives of his society. Violent emotions related to conflict—these are the most absorbing of our more private experiences; and the most enduringly popular works of art are always those which stir up such emotions. Bad, exciting art has always been good enough for the majority; the more civilized minority demands stimulants of a subtler, richer and more elegant kind. Today the majority can get what it wants from whodunits and the popular press. The minority professes to be shocked because the majority's favourite newspapers give so much space to crimes of violence, such tall headlines to any kind of sexual scandal. But from its first invention, crimes of violence and sexual scandal have been the subject matter of drama. Stripped of their poetry the plots of all the world's great tragedies are simply items from the front page of the *Police Gazette*.

In high tragedy as in low journalism there is no room for the dispassionate observations, the marshalled data and logical thinking of science. This incompatibility

56

reflects the huge historical fact of humanity's never ending civil wars—the wars between reason and the instincts, reason and the passions, reason and rationalized unreason, reason in the guise of enlightened self-interest and the criminal lunacies that sanctify themselves as idealism and get organized as religions, moralities and public policy. From age to age this civil war remains forever the same; but its manifestations change with changing circumstances. Thus in the Age of Faith the much-touted essence of Christian unity was qualified (to use the language of the Schools) by the observable accidents, throughout Christendom, of almost incessant mutual throat-cutting. Today, on either side of the Iron Curtain, we are all humanists. Ours is the Age of the Welfare State. It is also the Age of Concentration Camps, Saturation Bombing and Nuclear Armaments. And, on the conceptual level, we live in an Age of Pure Science and Analytical Philosophy that is, at the same time and even more characteristically, an Age of Nationalistic Idolatry, Organized Lying and Non-Stop Distractions.

> Surely, it's obvious.
> Doesn't every schoolboy know it?
> Ends are ape-chosen: only the means are man's.
> Papio's procurer, bursar to baboons,
> Reason comes running, eager to ratify . . .
> Comes with the Calculus to aim your rockets
> Accurately at the orphanage across the ocean;
> Comes, having aimed, with incense to impetrate
> Our Lady devoutly for a direct hit.

In this civil war the literary artist finds himself qualified by his special talents to play two important parts—that of war correspondent and that of propagandist. As the professional recorder of man's more private experiences, he observes the various manifestations of unreason, negative and positive, conceptualized or in the raw, and can see how they are related to the public world of social organizations and philosophical systems. Moreover, possessing as he does a special gift for purifying words, he is in a position to make effective propaganda for either of the two combatants. Will he range himself with reason in the service of Decency? Or with rationalization in the service of the Immanent Baboon? Is he using his gifts to work for more life, more love, more freedom? Or does he

> Come, a catch-fart with Philosophy, truckling to tyrants,
> Come, a pimp for Prussia, with Hegel's patent History?

He is free—freer than most people, for most people are inescapably enmeshed in some powerful social organization—to make the choice.

Many writers have, as a matter of plain historical fact, made the wrong choice. Again and again, genius and reputation have been placed at the disposal of Power, Vested Interest and Rationalized Unreason. 'Time' (as W. H. Auden writes in his admirable poem on the death of Yeats),

> Time that is intolerant
> Of the brave and innocent,
> And indifferent in a week
> To a beautiful physique.
>
> Worships language and forgives
> Everyone by whom it lives;
> Pardons cowardice, conceit,
> Lays its honours at their feet.

Time that with this strange excuse
Pardoned Kipling and his views,
And will pardon Paul Claudel,
Pardons him for writing well.

Hamlet and *Agamemnon* are as full of horrors as the tabloids; but because Shakespeare and Aeschylus gave a purer sense to the words of their respective tribes, we forgive them and at the same time forgive ourselves, as we listen to those marvellous words, for enjoying the violent emotions which their renderings of homicide and sexual scandal so powerfully evoke.

Science is a matter of disinterested observation, un-prejudiced insight and experimentation, patient ratiocination within some system of logically correlated concepts. In real-life conflicts between reason and passion the issue is uncertain. Passion and prejudice are always able to mobilize their forces more rapidly and press the attack with greater fury; but in the long run (and often, of course, too late) enlightened self-interest may rouse itself, launch a counter-attack and win the day for reason. In the fictional world of the drama, this is not likely to happen. To begin with, we go to the tragic theatre in order to be excited, go for the express purpose of vicariously living through the violent feelings associated with crime and sexual scandal. If there is to be any talk about reason and disinterested awareness, any reference to science as information, science as theory and science as a basis of a general philosophy, it must come in the course of digressions from the main theme of emotion-arousing conflict. But plays are short and the art of telling a story and describing characters in dramatic terms is long. The author of a tragedy has little time, and his audience even less patience, for digressions from the emotion-arousing situations which are the substance of all high drama. In comedy the conflicts are less irreconcilable and the feelings aroused, less violent. Digressions, in consequence, seem less digressive and are listened to, not merely in patience, but with positive pleasure. That supreme master of dramatic digression, Bernard Shaw, enjoyed an enormous popularity. (It should be remarked, incidentally, that Shaw used his mastery to talk a good deal of eloquent nonsense about Darwinian biology and, in his *Black Girl*, Pavlovian psycho-physiology.)

24

The novel and the essay are art forms far more tolerant of digressions than comedy even at its most conversational. Provided the writing is good enough, most things can be said in an essay and practically anything, from the most intensely private of subjective experiences to the most public of observations and reasonings, can find its place in a novel. We see then, that in poems and tragedies scientific reference can only be slight. There is more scope for it in comedy, but not nearly so much scope as in the essay or the three hundred-page narrative.

I am not qualified, nor in this context is it necessary for me, to write a comprehensive History of Scientific Reference in Literature. Our main concern is not with the past, but with the present and the immediate future. Whether we like it or not, ours is the Age of Science. What can a writer do about it? And what, as a conscientious literary artist and a responsible citizen, ought he to do about it?

First and most important, the writer must perform to the best of his ability the tasks for which his talents uniquely qualify him—namely, to render, in words purer

60

than those of the tribe, his own and other people's more private experiences; to relate these experiences in some humanly satisfying way to public experiences in the universes of natural facts, linguistic symbols and cultural conventions; and to get on with the job of making the best of all the worlds in which human beings are pre-destined to do their living and their dying, their perceiving, feeling and thinking. Literature gives a form to life, helps us to know who we are, how we feel and what is the point of the whole unutterably rummy business. Our immediate experiences come to us, so to say, through the refracting medium of the art we like. If that art is inept or trivial or over-emphatic, our experiences will be vulgarized and corrupted. Along with unrealistic philosophy and religious superstition, bad literature is a crime against society.

Schizophrenics live almost exclusively in the world of private experience; but for healthy people, their private world is always experienced, or at least thought about, in relation to a number of public worlds. Large areas of this public domain have been mapped and systematically described, on every conceptual level from the sub-atomic to the biological and the psychological, by men of science. How should the literary artist relate himself to this hierarchy of scientific domains?

The pre-condition of any fruitful relationship between literature and science is knowledge. The writer, whose primary concern is with purer words and the more private of human experiences, must learn something about the activities of those who make it their business to analyse man's more public experiences and to co-ordinate their findings in conceptual systems described in purified words of another kind—the words of precise definition and logical discourse. For the non-specialist, a thorough and detailed knowledge of any branch of science is impossible. It is also unnecessary. All that is necessary, so far as the man of letters is concerned, is a general knowledge of science, a bird's eye knowledge of what has been achieved in the various fields of scientific enquiry, together with an understanding of the philosophy of science and an appreciation of the ways in which scientific information and scientific modes of thought are relevant to individual experience and the problems of social relationships, to religion and politics, to ethics and a tenable philosophy of life. And, it goes without saying, between the Two Cultures the traffic of learning and understanding must flow in both directions—from science to literature, as well as from literature to science.

'*Je crois peu*,' said Victor Hugo, '*à la science des savants bêtes.*' His scepticism was understandable, but not, as we shall see, justifiable. The number of *savants bêtes* is very considerable, and growing all the time. Here is what an able scientist, Dr J. Gillis of the Weizman Institute in Israel, has to say on this subject. 'Let us face the facts. A large number of young people take up scientific research as a career these days, but regrettably few are impelled into it by a passionate curiosity as to the secrets of nature. For the vast majority it is a job like any other job. . . . Moreover it is not generally realized outside of academic circles how far a mediocre research worker can get. With the exception of pure mathematics nearly all scientific research is now done by teams, and the spectrum of ability of teams members can be very wide—and flat. Indeed one can hold a respected job and even make a worthwhile contribution to the world by having sufficient intelligence to do what one is told . . . and the devotion required to come to work on time and perform it honestly. In commerce and industry there are those who are exceptionally endowed with brilliance, ruthlessness or luck and achieve proportionate success; then come the vast majority who somehow manage to get through, and the minority who go under. The proportion of scientists who actually go under is probably much lower and the weeding out process is correspondingly less effective. Indeed the relative security and stability of the research career are probably more attractive to mediocrities than the romance of enquiry is to the brilliant ones. And without this great intellectual proletariat of research how far should we get?'

A century ago the intellectual proletariat of research was but a tiny fraction of the vast intellectual proletariat of research today. But it was evidently large enough, even then, to have attracted Victor Hugo's attention. The *savant bête* was one of the phenomena of modern life which that consummate journalist, the author of *Choses Vues*, had clearly recognized, and to which the poet-turned-philosopher reacted by refusing to believe in the correctness of stupid people's findings. We who are contemporary with the explosive growth in numbers of the intellectual proletariat of research can admire the sharp-eyed journalist and sympathize with the poet-philosopher. But since we are also contemporary with an unprecedentedly rapid advance in science and technology, we have to recognize the fact that, though understandable, the poet-philosopher's scepticism was unjustified. Victor Hugo thought that, like creativity in literature, creativity in science was entirely dependent on individual talent. And of course it is still true that revolutionary advances in scientific thinking and experimentation are made by outstanding individuals. But these break-throughs into new territory require to be consolidated and widened; and for this task a force of intellectual proletarians is necessary and, provided they obey the rules of the scientific game, qualitatively adequate. One of the great achievements of science is to have developed a method which works almost independently of the people by whom it is operated. Men and women with only enough intelligence to do what they are told and only the devotion required to come to work on time can, by using the method, extend and apply scientific knowledge. These members of the intellectual proletariat of research are *savants bêtes*, much less interesting than successful professionals in other fields; but the method they use is a sufficient substitute for personal ability.

25

In the hierarchy of the sciences, atomic physics is the most exact, the most completely expressible in terms of mathematics, and the most remote from immediate experience. For the writer, atomic physics is interesting, above all, for the way in which it illustrates the workings of the scientific mind as it moves from a set of sense perceptions to a set of unobservable, hypothetical entities and back again to another set of sense perceptions, in relation to which the concepts of the atomic hypothesis are operationally validated. In the words of an eminent physicist, Werner Heisenberg, 'for the first time in history man, on this planet, is discovering that he is alone with himself, without a partner and without an adversary'. To put it more picturesquely, man is in process of becoming his own Providence, his own Cataclysm, his own Saviour and his own invading horde of Martians. And in the realm of pure science the same discovery—that he is alone with himself —awaits him as he progressively refines his analysis of matter. 'Modern science,' says Heisenberg, 'shows us that we can no longer regard the building blocks of matter, which were considered originally to be the ultimate objective reality, as being things "in themselves" . . . Knowledge of atoms and their movements "in themselves", that is to say independent of our observation, is no longer the aim of research; rather we now find ourselves from the very start in the midst of a dialogue between nature and man, a dialogue of which science is only one part, so much so that the conventional division of the world into subject and object, into inner world and outer world, into body and soul, is no longer applicable and raises difficulties. For the sciences of nature, the subject matter of research is no longer nature in itself, but nature subjected to human questioning, and to this extent man, once again, meets only with himself'.

To the literary artist who has been concerned with man's more private experiences, this talk about the inappropriateness of the conventional notions of objective and subjective, outer and inner, has a familiar ring. It reminds him of certain utterances of the poets and the mystics. Carried far enough, the analysis of man's public experiences comes, in theory at least, to the same conclusion as is reached existentially in the most private of all private experiences—infused contemplation, *samadhi*, *satori*.

26

Satori, *samadhi*, infused contemplation—how many questions, literary, scientific and philosophical, cluster about these words! For example, what kind of purified language will be required to do justice to an experience which may be 'explained' equally well in terms of ancient poetical paradoxes, or of the latest neuro-pharmacology? Zen or psilocybin? Patanjali or Dr What's-his-name of I forget which Mental Hospital? Unrepeatable experiences communicated in the purified, many-meaninged words of literature, or a logically coherent, jargonized discourse, made up of words with only a single meaning, about the similarities between unique events, the common factors in reported experiences, the average of observed behaviours. A literary artist with a survey-knowledge of the relevant sciences and an enormous gift of language will no doubt find a way to make the best of both worlds. And attacking the same problem from their side of the spiritual Iron Curtain, the scientists should also look for ways to make the best of both worlds. At present all too many scientists, especially the *savants bêtes* of research's intellectual proletariat, seem to think that theories based upon the notion of 'nothing-but' are somehow more scientific than theories consonant with actual experience, and based upon the principle of not-only-this-but-also-that. For example, to call psilocybin a 'psychotomimetic agent' and to equate the experiences it induces with those of certifiable lunatics, is regarded as being thoroughly 'scientific'. To call it a 'psychodelic', or soul-revealing, agent and to point out that the psilocybin experience is felt by most subjects to be uniquely significant and that its effects are often enlightening and transforming—this is felt to be dangerously 'unscientific'. If the *savants bêtes* had their poet, he would tell them, no doubt, that 'We needs must love the lowest when we see it', and must also be very careful to shut our eyes to everything except the lowest. The intelligent scientist who pays attention to his own private experiences and has read what others report of theirs, will find himself in agreement with the intelligent writer, who has paid attention to what the scientists have to say about public experiences. Together, they will work for the creation of a comprehensive philosophy in which it will be obvious that, while high can always be reduced to low, low can always emerge into high; a philosophy that will analyse and classify, but make it clear, at the same time, that analysis and classification, though absolutely necessary, must never be taken too seriously and that in spite of science, in spite of the notions of 'common sense' imposed upon us by the vocabulary, grammar and syntax of our unpurified language, reality remains for ever whole, seamless and undivided.

27

Biology, it is obvious, is more immediately relevant to human experience than are the exacter sciences of physics and chemistry. Hence, for all writers, its special importance. The sciences of life can confirm the intuitions of the artist, can deepen his insights and extend the range of his vision. Writers, spiritual directors, men of affairs—'all these people', writes Professor A. H. Maslow, 'may have wonderful insights, ask the questions that need to be asked, put forth challenging hypotheses, and may even be correct and true much of the time. But however sure *they* may be, they can never make mankind sure. . . . Science is the only way we have of shoving truth down the reluctant throat. Only science can overcome characterological differences in seeing and believing. Only science can progress'.

The sciences of life have need of the artist's intuitions and, conversely, the artist has need of all that these sciences can offer him in the way of new materials on which to exercise his creative powers. And humanity at large—the race of multiple amphibians, uneasily living at one and the same moment in four or five different and disparate universes—has need of the syntheses which only the man of letters with 'a heart that watches and receives' and a bird's-eye knowledge of science can provide. Such fusions of public and private, of fact and value, of conceptual knowledge and immediate experience, of scientifically purified discourse and the purer words of literature, are possible in every domain accessible to perception, feeling and thought.

The proper study, or at least one of the properest studies, of mankind is man. What have poets, dramatists, story tellers and philosophical essayists contributed to this study in the past? What are scientists contributing now? And what should be the attitude of the twentieth-century man of letters toward these scientific contributions to the study of man? How can he make use of them, improve upon them, incorporate them into works of literary art?

28

The word 'man' is currently used in at least three principal senses. Thus it may stand for humanity at large, for the whole species as it now exists on this planet. Or it may stand, rather vaguely, for an average of people's behaviour within some specified culture at some particular period of history. We speak, for example, of Primitive Man, Classical Man, Western Man, Post-Historic Man, and so forth. The cultural varieties of *Homo sapiens* are almost as numerous as the breeds of dogs and almost as dissimilar. And finally the word, 'man', may refer to the unique individual, to any one of the three thousand million human anatomies and physiologies, the three thousand million *loci* of private and unshareable experience, now extant.

Until very recent times even the best-informed of philosophers and literary artists knew nothing about man-the-species, and very little about man-the-product-of-culture. The earth was largely unexplored, archaeology had not been invented and such historians as existed were the chroniclers of local events, whose ignorance of all but a very few alien cultures was complete. Virtually everything we now know about ourselves as the resultants of evolution, as the earth's dominant, wildly proliferating and most destructive species, as the creators, beneficiaries and victims of culture, as the genius-inventors and idiot-dupes of language, has come to us, during the last three or four generations, from palaeontologists and ecologists, from systematic historians and, in all their variety, from the social scientists. And from geneticists, neurologists and bio-chemists has come, in great measure during the present century, most of what we now know about human beings as members of the animal kingdom, as living organisms with an inherited anatomy and an inherited chemical and temperamental individuality. Some of this new knowledge—especially the new social, linguistic and historical knowledge—has been built into the frame of reference, within which men of letters, along with most of their contemporaries, perceive, feel, think and express themselves. The rest, to a great extent, still remains outside the pale of literature, unassimilated by those whose traditional function it is to study man as unique person, culture-product and species, and to communicate their findings—their 'criticism of life', in

Arnold's phrase—in the purified language of literary art.

29

Who are we? What is our destiny? How can the often frightful ways of God be justified? Before the rise of science, the only answers to these questions came from the philosopher-poets and poet-philosophers. Thus, in India the engima of man's individual and collective destiny was unriddled in terms of a theory—implausibly simple and suspiciously moralistic—of re-incarnation and *karma*. Present good luck was the reward for past virtue, and if you were suffering now, it was your fault—you had sinned in a previous existence. Liberation from the endlessly turning wheel of birth and death, the everlasting succession of do-it-yourself heavens and strictly home-made hells—this is the goal of life, the ultimate reason for human existence.

In the Christian West the riddle was solved (or perhaps it would be truer to say that it was re-stated) in terms of some completely unobservable act of supernatural predestination—an act for which no logical and even, in the absence of a belief in reincarnation, no ethically acceptable reason could be given. It was a matter simply of the arbitrariness of omnipotence, of God's good pleasure.

Man's destiny is a matter, among other things, of the observable differences between human individuals. Are these differences inherited or acquired, or inherited *and* acquired? For many centuries it seemed reasonable to debate the problem of Nature versus Nurture in terms of theology and metaphysics. Augustinians fought with Pelagians; proto-Behaviourists, such as Helvétius, reacted against Jansenist Christianity by maintaining, in the teeth of all probability and on no evidence whatever, that any shepherd boy from the Cevennes could be transformed, by suitable tutoring, into another Isaac Newton or (if the tutor preferred) into a replica of St Francis of Assisi. 'Everything', said Rousseau, 'is good that comes from the hands of the Creator; everything is perverted by the hands of man.' The Creator is now out of fashion; but environmental determinism remains the frame of reference within which many social scientists and many men of letters still do their feeling and their thinking. Theirs, surely, is an inexcusable one-sidedness; for the science of genetics has been with us for a long life-time and the unscientific study of innate human differences is as old as literature. At no period and in no place would any dramatist or story-teller in his right mind have dreamed of clothing the character, say, of Falstaff in the physique of Hotspur, or the temperament of Mr Pickwick in the body of Uriah Heep.

The beginnings of a science of human destiny (in so far as our destiny depends upon our innate idiosyncrasies) are to be found in the humoural theories of Greco-Roman medicine. Men are alike inasmuch as all human bodies secrete the four humours. Their dissimilarities result from the fact that these humours are mixed in different proportions. Disease results from a temporary upsetting of the normal balance of the humours. Congenitally, everyone has his own unique temperament or mixture of humours. When the mixture is altered, there is distemper. (This last word has come down in the world. In the sixteenth century even a king could be distempered. Today, for some odd historical reason, distemper is the name exclusively of a disease of dogs and cats.)

Ben Jonson's dramatic typology was based upon the most advanced scientific theories of his age. They were crude theories, and for this reason Ben's characters seem less real, less fully human, than do those of his less scientific contemporary, the creator of Falstaff and Cleopatra.

It was not until the twentieth century that science at last caught up with literature and began to correlate differences of physique with differences of temperament and behaviour. What the men of letters had done intuitively was now done methodically by the experimenters and the statisticians. On the level of anatomy, genetic predestination was studied by Kretschmer, Stockard, and William Sheldon; on the bio-chemical level, by Roger Williams and, in relation to the insane, by Hoffer, Osmond, Heath, Altdorf and numerous workers in Russia and Czechoslovakia. It is now clear that a propensity to schizophrenia, and perhaps to other forms of severe mental illness as well, is innate. So too are certain propensities to the kind of behaviour that we describe as delinquent. *Crime as Destiny* was the title of a book (published in English, with an introduction by J. B. S. Haldane, in 1930) in which Johannes Lange summarized the results of his work on pairs of identical and identically criminal twins. Twenty years later a correlation between delinquent behaviour and certain inherited patterns of physique and temperament was established by the researches of Sheldon and the Gluecks.

Manners maketh man, but on the other hand *you can't make a silk purse out of a sow's ear*. The old proverbs flatly contradict one another, but are both correct. Predestined by their heredity, human beings are post-destined by their environment. A mildly bad predestination may be

72

offset by a more than averagely good post-destination; but even the best of post-destinations has never as yet shown itself capable of nullifying the effects of a very bad predestination.

From individual *karma* we now pass to the enigma of collective destiny. Kipling was probably wrong in asserting that there were lesser breeds without the law. But, along with many other observers, he was probably right in thinking that the manifest differences between racial temperaments were more than merely cultural and must be due, at least in part, to hereditary factors.

This intuitive hunch has received a measure of scientific confirmation from the recent research into the relationship between blood types and temperament carried out by the French anthropologist and psychologist, Léone Bourdel. In a given collectivity the predominance of one or other of the four blood types—A, B, O and AB—is a kind of immanent social destiny. For example, peoples with a relative predominance in their population of B-blood 'are by nature the most spontaneously warlike'. Again, 'wherever A's and B's confront one another in sufficient numbers, friction instantly arises. The clash is between two contrasting ways of life, two biological rhythms, two metaphysics, two modes of government, irreducibly different in each case one from the other'. An A-type temperament being irreducibly different from a B-type temperament, it follows that AB individuals grow up to be the victims of a built-in *angoisse psychologique*. Furthermore, societies with a predominance of AB's in their population are foredoomed to an existence of chronic restlessness, a history of permanent revolution. (AB peoples, we are told, inhabit the Balkans, the lands of the Near East, Central America and the northern part of South America.)

To the twentieth-century man of letters science offers a treasure of newly discovered facts and tentative hypotheses. If he accepts this gift and if, above all, he is sufficiently talented and resourceful to be able to transform the new raw materials into works of literary art, the twentieth-century man of letters will be able to treat the age-old, and perennially relevant theme of human destiny with a depth of understanding, a width of reference, of which, before the rise of science, his predecessors (through no fault of their own, no defect of genius) were incapable.

30

The ways of God have never been justified, but they can be explained, at least partially, in non-theological terms. Why do these things happen to us? As we have seen, a number of fragmentary, but nonetheless useful and even enlightening answers to the riddle of human destiny are now forthcoming. And the same thing is true of the closely related riddle of human nature. Who or what are we? A complete scientific answer to this question is still lacking. We know a great deal, but we do not yet know how to correlate what we know into an explanation. In the words of a very able contemporary psychologist, Dr H. J. Eysenck, 'we have no recognized hypothesis to account for the apparent interaction of mind and matter in a simple act of consciousness, nor is there any official hypothesis to account for the phenomena of hypnosis or of memory'.

What we do have, however, is a great mass of facts unco-ordinated in terms of a comprehensive theory, but intrinsically interesting, suggestive, speculation-provoking —such stuff, in a word, as literature is made of. Who are we, and how did we come to be what we are? From age to age the makers of literature have proposed an answer to this question in terms of whatever factual observations, whatever explanatory notions, passed in their time for scientific. Going back to the beginnings of our own literary tradition, we find that, in Homer's day, a human being had no unitary soul. His psyche was merely the shadowy thing that feebly squeaked and gibbered in the world of the dead. In the world of the living a human being was simply an uneasily co-operative society of somato-psychic factors—a parliament in which the nominal prime minister, Nous or Reason, was constantly being outvoted by the spokesmen of the opposition parties of Animal Vitality, Emotion and Instinct. And it was not merely with Phren, Thumos and the Liver that Reason had to cope; there were also the gods. Supernatural intervention was constant and generally malicious. One of Zeus's numerous daughters was Até, whose name, in the Homeric poems, means 'the state of mind-body that leads to disaster'. Até amused herself by playing havoc with rational man's best-laid plans and noblest intentions. And when it wasn't Até who made the mischief, it was one of the high gods personally intervening, so that some unfortunate human being might suffer undeserved pain or perpetrate some act of suicidal idiocy.

But divine interventions were not invariably malicious. Inspiration by one or other of the Muses was an actual experience, and from time to time some god or other would intervene to help one of his favourites. Moreover there was something called Menos, the state of mind-body that leads to success. Entering a man, Menos enormously

75

increased his native capacities, making it possible for him to achieve what had hitherto been impossible.

Homer's analysis of human nature makes us smile. But let us never forget that, although less knowledgeable than we, our ancestors were no stupider. Consider, for example, those odd and embarrassing events, about which we now think in terms of a number of moderately scientific hypotheses—a hypothesis of innate instinctual drives, a hypothesis of neurotic obsessions and hysterical inhibitions, a hypothesis of conditioned reflexes, habit formation and learning, and a hypothesis of inherited or acquired bio-chemical anomalies. By those to whom they happen these odd events are commonly experienced as gradual or sudden invasions of the self by irresistibly powerful forces from some alien 'out there', which is yet within us. For this reason, the most obvious and plausible explanation of some of the very peculiar things we feel, think, say and do is an explanation in terms of a comprehensive theory of supernatural intervention. Indeed, before the systematic accumulation of physiological and psychological facts, and the formulation of working hypotheses based upon those facts, no other theory of human nature was able to 'save the appearances'. The hypothesis that human beings are subject to assaults and possessions by supernatural entities remained the only adequate explanation of man's observed behaviour until, in very recent times, naturalistic theories of psycho-chemical interaction, of learning and conditioning, and of a dynamic unconscious, were developed to take its place.

Contact with Indian gymnosophists to the east or, as some contemporary scholars believe, contact to the north with the shamans of the Central Asiatic steppes led to the abandonment of the Homeric view of human nature. The

debating society of somato-psychic factors gave place to
the dualism of a soul, confined, as in a penitentiary or a
tomb, within a body, whose inert matter it informed and
animated. The notion of a detachable psyche imprisoned
in a muddy and decaying soma gave birth to the notions
of original sin and concurrently of an undiluted spiritu-
ality, to which there could be no access save through a
course of physical mortifications. Orphism and the
Pythagoreans prepared the way for Plato and, reinforced
by Persian dualism, the new theory of human nature
entered our cultural history on the carrying wave of
Christianity. Mediaeval theology enriched this theory of
human nature by incorporating into it the hypotheses
of Aristotelian science. Vegetative, animal and rational,
the soul was a trinity in unity; and this trinity in unity
informed a body which was a variously mingled four-in-
one of hot, cold, moist and dry, of sanguine, phlegmatic,
choleric and melancholic. This mediaeval threesome
within a foursome was even more liable than the old
somato-psychic debating society had been to supernatural interventions. To Homeric superstition, Persians,
Jews and Christians had added their repulsive phantasies
of unremitting assaults by innumerable fiends, of diabolic
infestations, of pacts between would-be magicians and
the denizens of that solidly material hell, in which,
according to the most reliable theologians, ninety-nine
hundredths of the human race were predestined to suffer
everlasting torment.

Eccentric as these old theories of human nature now
seem, the fact remains that they worked. Guided by the
traditional anthropology and their own intuitions, our
ancestors managed to survive, to make technological
progress, to create viable social organizations and splendid

works of art. Only too frequently, it is true, they took their theories too seriously, mistook poetical fancies for established truths, picturesque metaphors for reality, the verbiage of philosophizing *littérateurs* for the word of God. When this happened, disasters inevitably followed. Obeying the dictates of an unrealistic anthropology and world-view, they embarked upon courses of personal and collective insanity—frightful self-torture and the equally frightful persecution of heretics; the repudiation of instinctual life and the sadistic torturing of wretched women accused of witchcraft; puritanism and the launching of crusades, the waging of hideously savage wars of religion. The notions *we* take too seriously are not the same as those which drove our fathers into their maniacal aberrations. But, though the causes differ, the results, at least on the collective level, are identical. Their unrealistic theories of man's nature and the nature of the world made it mandatory for them to bully, persecute and kill—always in the name of God. We too kill, persecute and bully, but not in order to propitiate Allah or to gratify the Holy Trinity. Our collective paranoia is organized in the name of the idolatrously worshipped Nation or the Divine Party. The misused notions, the overvalued words and phrases are new; but the resultant slaughters and oppressions are dismally familiar. Science, it seems hardly necessary to remark, provides no justification for slaughter and oppressions. Hand in hand with progressive technology, it merely provides the means for implementing the old insanities in a novel and more effective way. The ends subserved by science are formulated in terms of what is most unscientific in our current view of the nature and potentialities of human beings, and of the point—the biological and psychological purpose, so

78

far as man-the-species and man-the-unique-person are concerned—of being alive and human. To keep drawing attention to this grotesque and increasingly dangerous state of affairs is surely one of the functions, one of the prime duties, of the twentieth-century man of letters.

31

We begin with the primitive monism of Homer's debating society of somato-psychic factors. We move on to the Scythian shamans, with their mediumistic techniques of 'travelling clairvoyance', and from shamanism to the Orphic, Pythagorean and Platonic theories of man as a detachable, autonomous unitary soul boxed up in a corporeal prison-tomb. From these we pass to the Christian hypothesis of man—a hypothesis that fluctuated between an almost Manichaean dualism and a kind of residual monism, expressing itself in the obscure eschatological doctrine of the resurrection of the body. Unmitigated dualism comes in with Descartes, and for more than two centuries remains the theory, in terms of which men of science and, with few exceptions, men of letters do their thinking about the human organism and its relationship to the external world. The nineteenth century witnessed the emergence of psychology as an independent science and of psychiatry as a medical speciality. The study of hypnosis revealed the interesting fact that many of the curious phenomena once attributed to supernatural intervention could be reproduced by suggestion or the 'magnetic passes', and could best be explained in terms of a theory of unconscious mental activity.

William James dated the birth of specifically modern psychology from the publication, in the early eighteen-eighties, of a paper by F. W. H. Myers, setting forth a theory (later developed at length in Myers' posthumous *Human Personality*) of the subliminal self. In 1895, after experimenting for some years with novel therapeutic techniques, Freud published his first book and formulated his famous theory of human behaviour in terms of libido, repression and a dynamic unconscious. Freud's hypothesis was less comprehensive than that of Myers; for, unlike his older English contemporary, he paid very little attention to what may be called the positive side of the unconscious. Myers was more interested in Menos than in Até; Freud's primary concern was with the state of mind that leads to disaster, not with the state of man that leads to success. As a research physician, with a large clientèle of hysterical and neurotic patients, he had ample opportunities for observing the destructive activities of Até, very few for observing the influxes of Menos, the visitations of the Muses, the phenomena of 'enthusiasm' (*en- theos*—God inside), or the admonitions of the kind of daimon that spoke to Socrates.

Freud's one-sided view of the unconscious was corrected by C. G. Jung—but corrected with a vengeance. Jung was interested in Menos; but he seems to have believed that Menos could do its beneficent work only by means of an enormous apparatus of symbols. Thanks to the inheritance of acquired characteristics, we are all born with a full supply of archetypes. For Jung, the unconscious was a populous mythological pantheon. Freud saw it rather as an underground urinal, scribbled over (for the symbols in which Freud was interested were almost exclusively sexual) with four-letter graffiti. Significantly enough, the patients of Freudian therapists regularly dream in Freudian symbols, whereas the patients of Jungian therapists always come up with archetypes. A neurotic is said to have achieved insight when, thanks to a steady bombardment of explicit or covert suggestions, he accepts his therapist's pet theory of human nature.

32

The Freudian hypothesis is open to criticism on many scores. It uses words which sound and read like scientific terms, but which are in fact not scientific at all, inasmuch as they have never been operationally defined. For example, the super-ego is supposed to be formed by the 'introjection' of the father figure into the child's unconscious mind. But the word 'introjection' is never defined in operational terms and so remains almost meaningless. And now let us consider the psycho-analytic interpretation of dreams. The proof that Freud's theory of dreams is correct resides in the fact that dream interpretation in terms of censorship and wish-fulfilment is in perfect accord with his fundamental theory of human nature. The correctness of the dream theory follows from the correctness of the fundamental hypothesis. And the fundamental Freudian hypothesis is proved to be correct by the fact that it is consonant with Freudian dream interpretation. Q.E.D.

To these logical deficiencies of the Freudian theory must be added its one-sidedness and an over-simplification of the problem under study by a wholesale and wholly unwarranted disregard of relevant facts. The hypothesis of unconscious mental activity is valid and of very great practical importance. Without it, we should be compelled to fall back on primitive notions of supernatural intervention. With it, we can offer partial explanations of some kinds of normal behaviour and can help some of the victims of the milder forms of mental illness to get rid of their symptoms. But to be adequate as a realistic explanation of the observed facts, and as a principle dictating therapeutic procedures, a merely psychological theory of human nature as a product of the interaction of conscious and unconscious mental activities, in relation to present and past environments, requires to be supplemented by other theories, based upon facts of a different order. Men and women are much more than the locus of conscious and unconscious responses to an environment. They are also unique, inherited patterns (within a unique, inherited anatomy) of biochemical events; and these patterns of bodily shape and cellular dynamics are in some way related to the patterns of an individual's mental activity. Precisely how they are related we do not know, for we have as yet no satisfactory hypothesis to account for the influence of matter upon mind and of mind upon matter. But the fact of their interaction has always been obvious, and a detailed knowledge of the fields in which bodily events determine and are in turn determined by mental events is steadily growing.

The basic Freudian hypothesis is an environmental determinism that ignores heredity, an almost naked psychology that comes very near to ignoring the physical correlates of mental activity. Freudian case histories very seldom contain a detailed description of the patient who is being treated. Is she one of those women who run to fat, or is she congenitally slender? Is he a driving mesomorph, or an over-sensitive, introverted ectomorph? We are not told. And yet every man of letters, from Homer's time to the present, has always known that the proper study of mankind can never be successful unless such questions are asked and conscientiously answered. And for every psychologist, scientific or intuitive, practical or

theoretical, it is no less important to know something
about the inner workings as well as the size and shape of
the body connected with a given set of mental activities.
But in orthodox Freudian literature bodies in their totality
are almost never discussed. True, the mouth and the anus
receive a good deal of attention—but after all, there is
nothing in between.

gnostic?
rejection
of body?

33

Because of all these grave weaknesses, orthodox Freudism
is giving way in therapy to an eclectic approach. There is
a growing recognition of the inescapable fact that men
and women are multiple amphibians inhabiting half a
dozen disparate universes at the same time. It is only by
attacking the problem of human nature on all its fronts—
the chemical and the psychological, the verbal and the
non-verbal, the individual, the cultural and the genetic—
that we can hope to understand it theoretically and to do
something about it in educational and therapeutic practice. Freud made significant contributions to the problem
of human nature on one sector of one front, the psychological. The results of his work are now in process of
being correlated with the results of work by other re-
searchers on other sectors of the same front, as well as on
many other fronts.

34

The scientific theory of human nature that is now emer-
ging is a good deal closer to the Homeric notion of a
debating society of somato-psychic factors than to the
more 'spiritual' hypothesis of an autonomous, unitary,
detachable soul imprisoned in a body, or the deceptively
commonsensical Cartesian notion of a soul attached,

somehow or other, to an automaton. A kind of prophetic summary of the new, non-Cartesian, non-Platonic view of man was given by William Blake in *The Marriage of Heaven and Hell*;

'All Bibles or sacred codes have been the causes of the following Errors.

1. That Man has two real existing principles, Viz: a Body and a Soul. *(not Hebrew)*

2. That Energy, call'd Evil, is alone from the Body, & that Reason, call'd Good, is alone from the Soul.

3. That God will torment Man in Eternity for following his Energies.

But the following Contraries to these are True.

1. Man has no Body distinct from his Soul; for that call'd Body is a portion of Soul discern'd by the five Senses, the chief inlets of Soul in this age.

2. Energy is the only life and is from the Body, and Reason is the bound or outward circumference of Energy.

3. Energy is Eternal Delight.'

This is not merely a forecast of future scientific findings; it is also a programme for a future literature. Thanks to the work in many fields of a host of scientific enquirers, thanks also to the philosophers of emergence and organization, the literary artist is now in a position to embark upon that programme. In Blake's day, body-soul convertibility was a hypothesis without a solid factual foundation and without adequate philosophical buttresses and superstructures. In ours, the basic information and the co-ordinating philosophy are there, waiting to be transfigured, challenging men of letters to purify the words of their tribe so as to make them capable of doing justice to a theory of human nature, subtler and more comprehensive than any of the theories elaborated by the philosopher-poets and proto-scientists of earlier centuries.

35

To think at once scientifically and artistically about the problems of manifold amphibiousness and multiple causation is difficult and laborious. It is much easier, much more wish-fulfilling, to think of human problems in terms of single causes and magically efficacious panaceas. That, no doubt, is why, in the recent past, men of letters have paid so much more attention to psycho-analysis than to the less spectacular, less pretentious, but more enlightening hypotheses contributed to the common store of scientific knowledge by physiologists and bio-chemists, by experimental psychologists, social scientists and anthropologists. The very fact that it was one-sided and over-simple made the Freudian hypothesis attractive. A more genuinely scientific hypothesis of human nature fails to attract precisely because it is genuinely scientific—because it refuses to over-simplify, but insists on doing justice to many aspects of an enormously complex reality.

In this context it is worth remarking that men of letters are ready to work very hard on obscure subjects of a non-scientific kind, but are not prepared to invest a comparable amount of labour in the artistic transfiguration of intrinsically less obscure scientific raw materials. Here, by way of example, are the opening lines of Ezra Pound's 'Near Perigord'

A Perigord, pres del muralh
Tan que i puosch' om gitar ab malh.

You'd have men's hearts up from the dust
And tell their secrets, Messire Cino,
Right enough? Then read between the lines of Uc St. Circ,
Solve me the riddle, for you know the tale.

And so the poem proceeds—Browning in modern dress, but a modern dress patched with bits of old Provençal, tagged and tasselled with all manner of mediaeval liripips. To catch the drift of what is being communicated, the average cultivated reader must work as hard on the quotations and historical allusions as he would have to work on the technical terms of an article in *Nature* or the *Archives of Neurology*.

Needless to say, there is no one-to-one correspondence between the merits of a work of literary art and the importance of its subject. Trivial events and commonplace ideas have served as the raw material for immortal writings. Conversely, in the hands of well-intentioned but untalented writers high themes turn into the flattest kind of literature. But where there is an equal display of talent, a good piece of literature dealing with some intrinsically interesting and important subject is surely preferable to a good piece of literature dealing with a subject of little interest and no importance. To me at least the facts recorded and the explanatory hypotheses put forth by scientific students of the age-old problem of man in his multiple amphibiousness seem particularly interesting and important—more interesting and more important than, for example, the mediaeval anecdote which is the theme of Mr Pound's poem. I admire the poem, but wish that its author, *il miglior fabbro* and consummate purifier of the words of the tribe, might have used his talents to transfigure some of the findings of modern science, thus making it possible for this new raw material to take its place, along with the traditional subject matters of poetry, in a work of the highest literary art.

Man, the multiple amphibian, lives in a chronic state of mild or acute civil war. The proper study of mankind is always a study of the 'fierce dispute betwixt damnation and impassioned clay', of that

> wearisome condition of humanity,
> Born under one law, to another bound;
> Vainly begot, and yet forbidden vanity;
> Created sick, commanded to be sound.

And Fulke Greville concludes his stanza with a question:

> What meaneth Nature by these diverse laws,
> Passion and reason, self-division's cause?

To the old answers, theological, metaphysical and palaeo-physiological, twentieth-century science has added answers of a different kind. The fierce dispute betwixt damnation and impassioned clay is now regarded as the expression of the fact that an ancient brain stem is associated with an overgrown, upstart cortex; that an endocrine system evolved for survival in the wild is built into the bodies of men and women living under conditions of complete domestication, in cages of words, within the larger confines of one or other of the cultural zoos. And for every individual the situation is complicated by the fact that he is anatomically and bio-chemically unique. His differences from other individuals are, for him, almost as important as his resemblances to them—in some cases, indeed, they are felt to be even more important. The explanatory hypotheses of modern science are not given to us in immediate experience. But neither were the explanatory hypotheses of theology and metaphysics. In this particular context, our immediate experience is only of the chronic civil war within ourselves, and of its consequences; anxiety, rage, frustration and so forth. Explanations in terms of God and Satan, of sin, conscience and categorical imperative, of *karma* and grace and predestination, are just as inferential, just as rationalistically public, as are the scientist's explanation in terms of evolution and neurology, of bio-chemical uniqueness at odds with cultural demands for uniformity.

An individual's reaction to a public hypothesis may be a private experience of great intensity. Thus, in the past, severe attacks of depression and suicidal despair were common among those tender-minded persons who took too seriously the hallowed notions of eternal punishment for sinners who had infringed the rules laid down by the local culture. Desolation as a subjective reaction to the public hypothesis of hell might give place to consolation as a subjective reaction to the public hypothesis of atonement. Analogously, subjective reactions to the public hypotheses of Lyellian geology and Darwinian biology took the form, in some individuals, of a joyous and entirely private sense of release from the shackles of ancient superstition, in others of a mournful sense of loss, an unshareable experience of being all alone in an unfriendly universe.

Subjective reactions to the hypotheses of human nature enunciated by modern science may take the form of private distress, private exultation, or private indifference —it is a matter of temperament and upbringing. The point to bear in mind is that, however unobservably inferential and rationally public, the scientific hypotheses of man in his multiple amphibiousness may very easily evoke, in a culture-conditioned mind, unshareable experiences of pleasure or distress, of forward-looking hope or nostalgic melancholy. In the past men of letters found it very easy to incorporate the all too humanly dramatic and picturesque hypotheses of theology and metaphysics into their poems, plays and narratives. Consider, for example, the perennially interesting topic of man's inner weather, with its sudden alterations of feeling tone, world-view and value judgments. How simple it was for George Herbert to relate these private experiences to the public doctrines of his Church! 'Who would have thought my shrivelled heart Could have recovered greenness?' he asks. But in fact, it *did* recover greenness, so that 'now in age I bud again; After so many deaths I live and write'.

> These are thy wonders, Lord of Power,
> Killing and quickening, bringing down to hell
> And up to heaven in an hour.

Again, 'how rich, O Lord, how fresh thy visits are!' (The words are from a lyric by Henry Vaughan)

> 'Twas but just now my bleak leaves hopeless hung,
>   Sullied with dust and mud. . . .
> But since thou didst in one sweet glance survey
> Their sad decays, I flourish and once more
>   Breathe all perfumes and spice.

In these two exquisitely beautiful poems private experience is harmonized with the public world-view of a religious philosophy that still regarded supernatural intervention as a sufficient explanation of unusual psychological happenings. For the twentieth-century man of letters this temptingly easy way out is barred. The only explanatory hypotheses that it is permissible to incorporate into a contemporary poem about changing moods are those of contemporary science. We have unshareably private experiences of alternating hell and heaven, of May

89

mornings eclipsed, from one moment to the next, into December midnights. Privately, these experiences *feel* as though they were the operations of some indwelling god or demon. But on the public level of rational inference, we have every reason to believe that they are the results of events taking place within the organism. We have learned that there is an endocrinology of elation and despair, a chemistry of mystical insight, and, in relation to the autonomic nervous sytem, a meteorology and even, according to Professor Piccardi, an astro-physics of changing moods.

The hypotheses of modern science treat of a reality far subtler and more complex than the merely abstract, verbal world of theological and metaphysical notions. And although a determinant of human nature and human behaviour, this reality is non-human, essentially undramatic, completely lacking in the obvious attributes of the picturesque. For these reasons it will be difficult to incorporate the hypotheses of science into harmonious, moving and persuasive works of art—much more difficult, obviously, than it was to incorporate the notions of diabolic obsession or of a Lord of Power arbitrarily quickening and killing the souls of His creatures. But for any serious and gifted artist a difficulty is never an insurmountable obstacle; it is a challenge to intellectual combat, a spur to further achievement. The conceptual and linguistic weapons with which this particular combat must be waged have not yet been invented. We do not know and, until some great artist comes along and tells us what to do, we shall not know how the muddled words of the tribe and the too precise words of the text books should be poetically purified, so as to make them capable of harmonizing our private and unshareable experiences with the scientific hypotheses in terms of which they are explained. But sooner or later the necessary means will be discovered, the appropriate weapons will be forged, the long-awaited pioneer of genius will turn up and, quite casually, as though it were the most natural thing in the world, point out the way. What that way will be, is of course completely unpredictable. To forecast what Shakespeare would do with the drama, a critic would have had to be another Shakespeare. In which case, needless to say, he would not have wasted his time talking about new kinds of literature; he would have made them.

36

The proper study of mankind is Man and, next to Man, mankind's properest study is Nature—that Nature of which <u>he is an emergent part</u> and with which, if he hopes to survive as a species, if he aspires to actualize the best of his individual and collective potentialities, he must learn to live in harmony. On this enormous theme what additional raw materials for the creation of new works of art can science bring to the man of letters?

Let us begin with ecology and its practical applications in the techniques of conservation, management of resources, pest control, breeding of resistant strains, hybridization and all the other arts by means of which man tries to maintain or, if it does not already exist, to create a satisfactory relationship with his natural environment. These arts and the accumulated facts and scientific theories upon which they are based, are not merely interesting in themselves; they are also profoundly significant for their ethical and philosophical implications. In the light of what we now know about the relationships of living things to one another and to their inorganic environment

—and also of what, to our cost, we know about over-population, ruinous farming, senseless forestry and des-tructive grazing, about water pollution, air pollution and the sterilization or total loss of productive soils—it has now become abundantly clear that the Golden Rule applies not only to the dealings of human individuals and human societies with one another, but also to their deal-ings with other living creatures and the planet upon which we are all travelling through space and time.

'Do as you would be done by.' Would we like to be well treated by Nature? Then we must treat Nature well. Man's inhumanity to man has always been condemned; and, by some religions, so has man's inhumanity to Nature. Not, however, by the religions which regard God as wholly Other, a Being apart from the created world. By these man's inhumanity to Nature is implicity condoned. Animals, said the theologians of Catholic orthodoxy, are without souls and may therefore be used as though they were things. The ethical and philosophical implications of modern science are more Buddhist than Christian, more Totemistic than Pythagorean and Platonic. For the eco-logist, man's inhumanity to Nature deserves almost as strong a condemnation as man's inhumanity to man. Not only is it profoundly wicked, and profoundly stupid, to treat animals as though they were things, it is also wicked and stupid to treat things as though they were *mere* things. They should be treated as though they were com-ponent parts of a living planetary whole, within which human individuals and human societies are tissues and organs of a special kind—sometimes, alas, horribly in-fected, riddled with proliferating malignancy.

For the Greeks of classical antiquity, *hubris*, that violent and overweening bumptiousness which is so

odiously characteristic of civilized humanity, was no less a
sin when directed against Nature than when directed
against one's fellow men. The essential soundness of their
ethical intuitions in this matter is attested by the findings
of contemporary science. So too is their feeling for moder-
ation in all things, their dislike of extremes and one-
sidedness. Nature, we now know, is a system of dynamic
balances, and when a state of equilibrium has been dis-
turbed, always attempts to establish a new balance between the forces involved. The ideal of the golden mean *naturalism*
has its roots in the natural order. Between some classes of
observed facts and some classes of felt values, certain
bridges are discernible. For the literary artist whose
properest study is Man, and whose next most proper study *2 worlds*
is Nature, the existence of such bridges is a matter of the
highest importance. On this middle ground between two
universes, traditionally regarded as completely disparate,
he will be able to discover the raw materials for a new
kind of Nature-literature.

37

Science sometimes builds new bridges between universes
of discourse and experience hitherto regarded as separate
and heterogeneous. But science also breaks down old
bridges and opens gulfs between universes that, traditionally, had been connected. Blake and Keats, as we have
seen, detested Sir Isaac Newton because he had cut the old
connections between the stars and the heavenly host,
between rainbows and Iris, and even between rainbows and Noah's Ark, rainbows and Jehovah—had
cut the connections and so de-poetized man's world
and robbed it of meaning. But in an age of science the
world can no longer be looked at as a set of symbols,

standing for things outside the world. *Alles Vergaengliche ist NICHT ein Gleichnis*. <u>The world is poetical intrinsically, and what it means is simply itself.</u> Its significance is the enormous <u>mystery</u> of its existence and of our awareness of that existence. Wordsworth's 'something far more deeply interfused, Whose dwelling is the light of setting suns, . . . and in the mind of man', is a deeper and more permanent foundation on which to build a life and a life-sustaining art than any traditional mythology.

But the myths are still there, still make their appeal to something in the mind of man—something, it is true, considerably more shifting, considerably less deeply interfused than the great nameless Something of Wordsworth's poem, but still psychologically important. The contemporary man of letters finds himself confronted, as he prepares to write about Nature, by a fascinating problem—the problem of harmonizing, within a single work of art, the old, beloved raw materials, handed down to him by the myth-makers of an earlier time, with the new findings and hypotheses now pouring in upon him from the sciences of his own day.

Let us consider this problem in terms of a particular case. In this second half of the twentieth century what should a literary artist, writing in the English language, do about nightingales? The first thing to be remarked is that the spraying of English hedgerows with chemical weed-killers has wiped out most of their population of assorted caterpillars, with the result that caterpillar-eating nightingales (along with caterpillar-eating cuckoos and those ex-caterpillars, the butterflies) have now become rarities in a land where they were once the most widely distributed of poetical raw materials.

There is subject matter here for a richly ramifying essay, a poem, at once lyrical and reflective, a long chapter in a Proustian novel. Thanks to science and technology we now have chemical sprays that kill the weeds in hedges. The sprays are used, the weeds are duly destroyed —and so is the biological basis of a long tradition of poetical feeling and poetical expression. Men must act, but should never forget that they are incapable of foreseeing the remoter consequences of their actions. No weeds, no caterpillars. No caterpillars, no Philomel with melody, no plaintive anthem or charming of magic casements. Our world is a place where nobody ever gets anything for nothing, where every gain in almost every field has to be paid for, either on the nail or in an indefinitely lengthy series of instalments.

Chemical sprays are not science's only contribution to the literary problem of the nightingale. Thanks to the bird watchers and the students of animal behaviour, we now know much more about the nightingale's song than was known in the past. The immortal bird (precariously *un*-immortal, as our recent experience with weed-killers has demonstrated) still sings, where the caterpillars are still sufficiently plentiful, its old, immemorially moving song. Darkling we listen,

> While thou art pouring forth thy soul abroad
> In such an ecstasy;

listen in the moonlight, while

> thick the bursts come crowding through the leaves.
> Again—thou hearest!
> Eternal Passion!
> Eternal pain!

And, as we listen, the old myths come back to mind

> Dost thou again behold,
> Here, through the moonlight on this English grass,
> The unfriendly palace in the Thracian wild?
>   Dost thou again peruse
> With hot cheeks and sear'd eyes
> The too clear web, and thy dumb Sister's shame?

Or else from the old Greek horror-story of crime, sexual scandal and miraculous interventions from on high, the listening poet may shift his attention to another beloved tradition. What he now hears is:

> Perhaps the self-same song that found a path
>   Through the sad heart of Ruth, when, sick for home,
>   She stood in tears amid the alien corn.

A century after Keats and half a century after Matthew Arnold, Mr T. S. Eliot made use of the same traditional raw material of English poetical feeling and poetical expression. He wrote of Philomel by the barbarous king

> So rudely forced; yet there the nightingale
> Filled all the desert with inviolable voice,
> And still she cries, and still the world pursues,
> 'Jug Jug' to dirty ears.

And how ingrainedly, how innately dirty those ears are! Sweeney's ears, Mrs Porter's ears, Rachel *née* Rabinovitch's ears. The nightingales, meanwhile,

> The nightingales are singing near
> The Convent of the Sacred Heart,

And sang within the bloody wood
When Agamemnon cried aloud,
And let their liquid siftings fall
To stain the stiff dishonoured shroud.

We are back among the ancient tales of crime and sexual scandal and supernatural intervention. In Mr Eliot's nightingale-literature, the only novelties are the dirtiness of the listening ears and the proximity of the Convent of the Sacred Heart. Agamemnon and the king of Daulis; Sweeney and Blessed Marguerite-Marie Alacoque, modern squalor, ancient barbarism and baroque religiosity—it is with these mythological upper partials, these cultural harmonics and satirical undertones that the song of the immortal bird comes to a great contemporary poet. From a reading of 'The Waste Land' and 'Sweeney Among the Nightingales' one would never suspect that Mr Eliot is a contemporary of Eliot Howard and Konrad Lorenz. When he speaks of Philomel he speaks of her as Arnold and Keats had spoken—as a creature with human feelings, singing her song within a merely cultural frame of reference. By the nineteen-twenties, when Mr Eliot was writing these poems, the reasons why birds sing were at last clearly understood. Howard and his fellow ethologists had discovered what Philomel's outpourings signified, what was their purpose. Man is the measure of all things. How true—for us! But for nightingales, the measure of the nightingale-universe is nightingales; the measure of a tiger's world is, for tigers, simply tigers. That the ethologists have been able to recognize this truth and to act upon it represents a major triumph of the scientific method. Philomel, it turns out, is not Philomel, but her mate. And when the cock-nightingale sings, it is not in pain, not in

97

passion, not in ecstasy, but simply in order to proclaim to other cock-nightingales that he has staked out a territory and is prepared to defend it against all comers. And, what makes him sing at night? A passion for the moon, a Baudelairean love of darkness? Not at all. If he sings at intervals during the night it is because, like all the other members of his species, he has the kind of digestive system that makes him want to feed every four or five hours throughout the twenty-four. Between caterpillars, during these feeding times, he warns his rivals (Jug, Jug, Jug) to keep off his private property.

When the eggs are hatched and territorial patriotism ceases to be necessary, a glandular change within the cock-nightingale's body puts a stop to all singing. Eternal pain and passion, the inviolable voice and the outpourings of ecstasy, give place to a silence, broken only by an occasional hoarse croak.

To the twentieth-century man of letters this new information about a tradition-hallowed piece of poetic raw material is itself a piece of potentially poetic raw material. To ignore it is an act of literary cowardice. The new facts about nightingales are a challenge from which it would be pusillanimous to shrink. And what a challenge! The words of the tribe and of the Text Book must be purified into a many-meaninged language capable of expressing simultaneously the truth about nightingales, as they exist in their world of caterpillars, endocrine glands and territorial possessiveness, and the truth about the human beings who listen to the nightingale's song. It is a strangely complex truth about creatures who can think of the immortal bird in strictly ornithological terms and who at the same time are overcome (in spite of ornithology, in spite of the ineradicable dirtiness of their ears) by the

98

magical beauty of that plaintive anthem as it fades 'past the near meadows, over the still stream'. It is truth about creatures who know perfectly well that everything transient is *not* a symbol of something else, but a part of whose mind likes to hark back to Philomela and the horrible tale of crime and counter-crime, of incestuous rape and avenging murder. It is a truth, finally, about creatures, in whose minds, far more deeply interfused than any scientific hypothesis or even any archetypal myth, is the Something whose dwelling is everywhere, the essential Suchness of the world, which is at once immanent and transcendent—'in here' as the profoundest and most ineffable of private experiences and at the same time 'out there', as the mental aspect of the material universe, as the emergence into cosmic mind of the organization of an infinity of organizations, perpetually perishing and perpetually renewed.

38

Thought is crude, matter unimaginably subtle. Words are few and can only be arranged in certain conventionally fixed ways; the counterpoint of unique events is infinitely wide and their succession indefinitely long. That the purified language of science, or even the richer purified language of literature should ever be adequate to the givenness of the world and of our experience is, in the very nature of things, impossible. Cheerfully accepting the fact, let us advance together, men of letters and men of science, further and further into the ever expanding regions of the unknown.

50-52 - area of poetry today is
same as Homer's area.